hello there!

There's a quiet joy in baking biscuits—the kind that fills your kitchen with warmth and turns everyday moments into something memorable. Simple & Sweet celebrates that joy with a collection of beautifully approachable recipes, perfect for everything from afternoon tea to last-minute gifts and cosy weekend bakes.

Inside, you'll find timeless favourites like buttery shortbread and jam-filled Linzers, seasonal treats, and quick bakes designed to impress with minimal fuss. Each recipe is made to be as lovely to look at as it is to share.

Whether you're baking for a celebration or simply indulging in a sweet moment of calm, Simple & Sweet invites you to slow down, put the kettle on, and enjoy the simple pleasure of something homemade.

Michelle

MY PASSION

A timeless collection of elegant, delicious cookies designed to bring warmth, joy, and beauty to your kitchen. Inside these pages, you'll discover classic favourites reimagined, delicate treats perfect for gifting, and simple recipes to make everyday moments feel special.

From buttery shortbread and jam-filled cookies to festive cookies and effortless bakes, this collection is crafted to inspire both seasoned bakers and beginners alike. Each recipe is approachable, beautiful, and made for sharing—because some of life's sweetest moments begin with a homemade cookie.

"Baking is love made visible—each biscuit is a simple reminder that the sweetest moments are the ones we share."

Table of
CONTENTS

01
Introduction

06-37
Timeless Classics

38-51
World-Famous Cookies

52-71
Biscuit Magic: Time-Saving Cookies

72-87
Festive and Seasonal Favorites

Table of CONTENTS

88-97
Chocolate Lovers Cookies

98-103
The Art of Gifting and Packaging

104-106
Must-Have Utensils

107-119
Handy Grocery List

120
Kitchen Conversions

122-125
The Sweetest Extras

126-127
Index

TIMELESS CLASSICS

There is a quiet and enduring charm in the timeless recipes we return to again and again. These biscuits bring comfort on afternoons, grace the table at family gatherings, and evoke memories of simpler, sweeter moments. In this collection of Timeless Classics, you'll find elegant and beloved bakes that have stood the test of time—recipes passed down through generations and lovingly reimagined for the modern baker.

From the delicate crumble of buttery shortbread to the jewel-like beauty of raspberry-filled window biscuits, each recipe captures the essence of traditional baking, emphasising refinement and simplicity. These biscuits are perfect for everyday indulgence, an elegant afternoon tea, or as thoughtful gifts that carry a sense of tradition and care.

Whether you are recreating a childhood favourite or discovering a new classic to make your own, this chapter celebrates the beauty of baking's most enduring treasures. Every recipe here is crafted to be reliable, delicious, and timeless—offering a sense of nostalgia while bringing joy to the present.

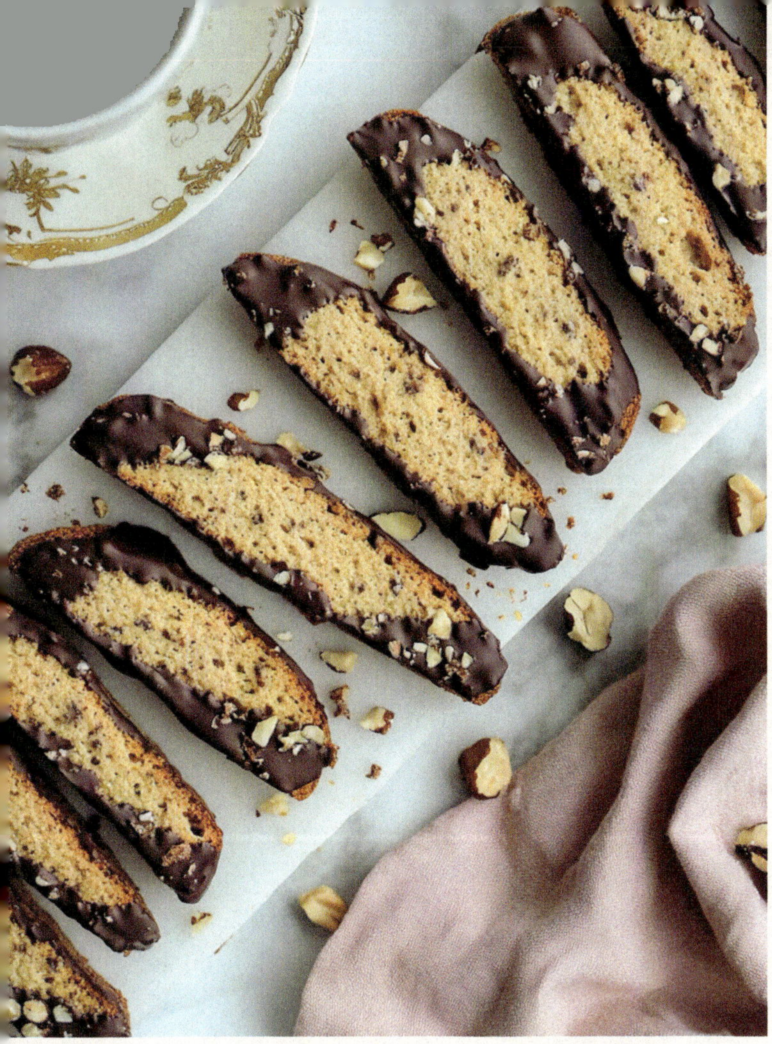
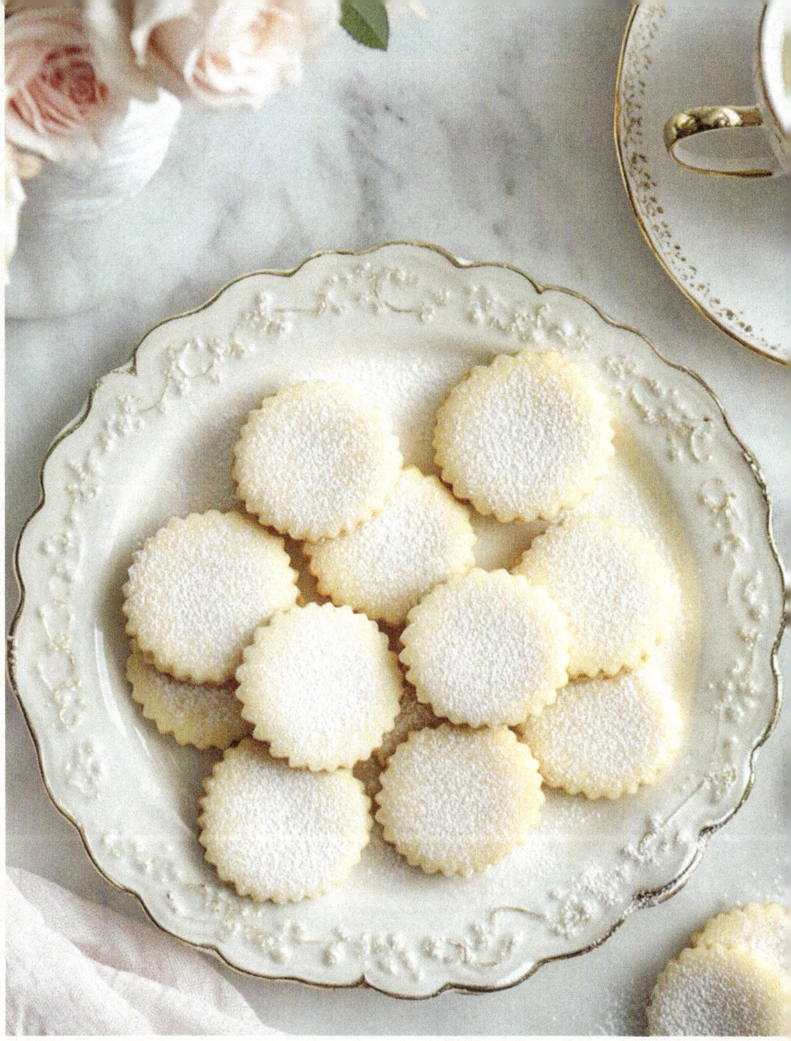
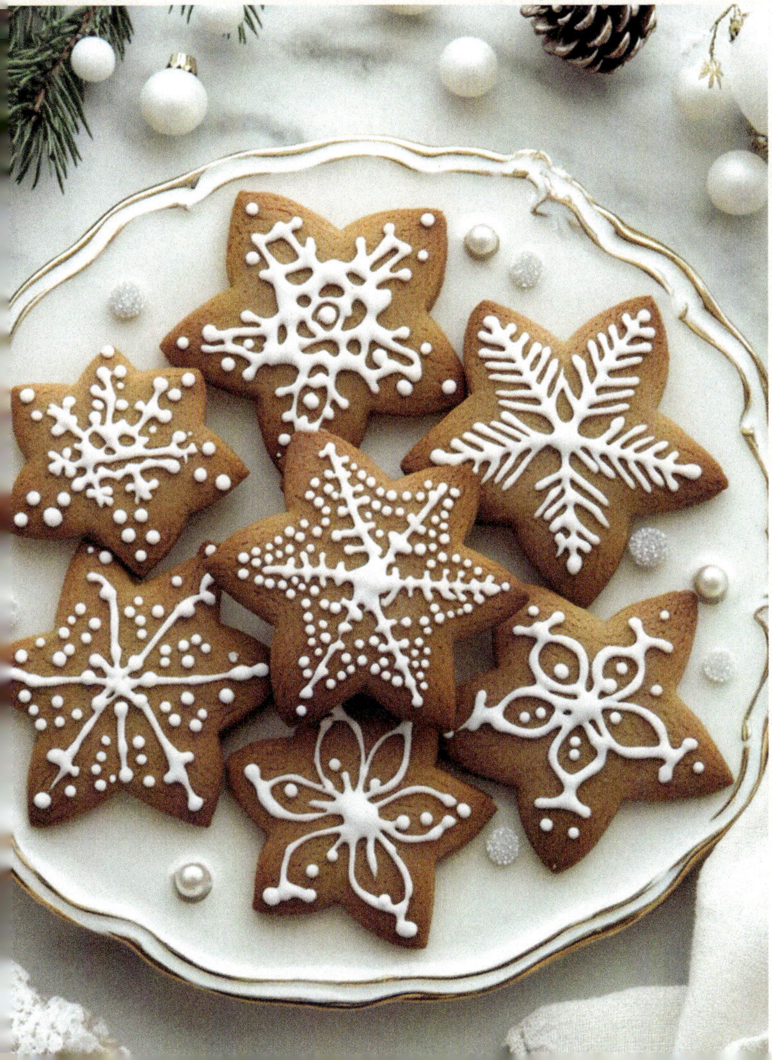
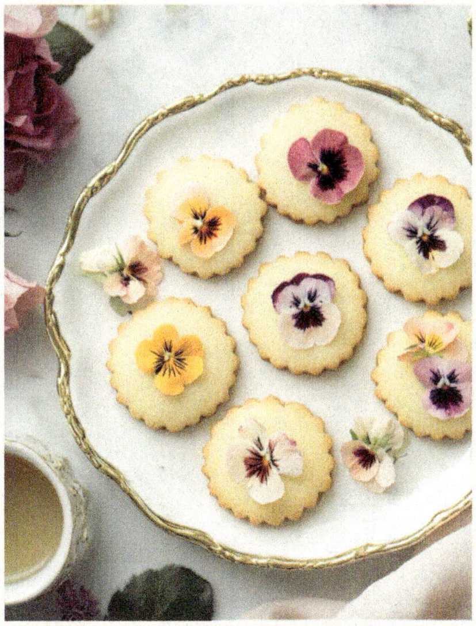
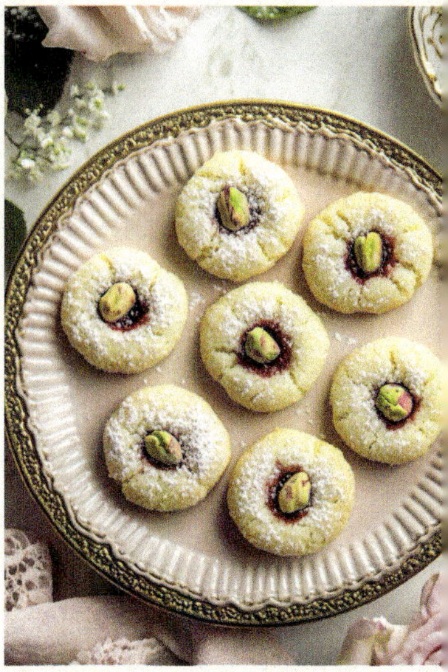
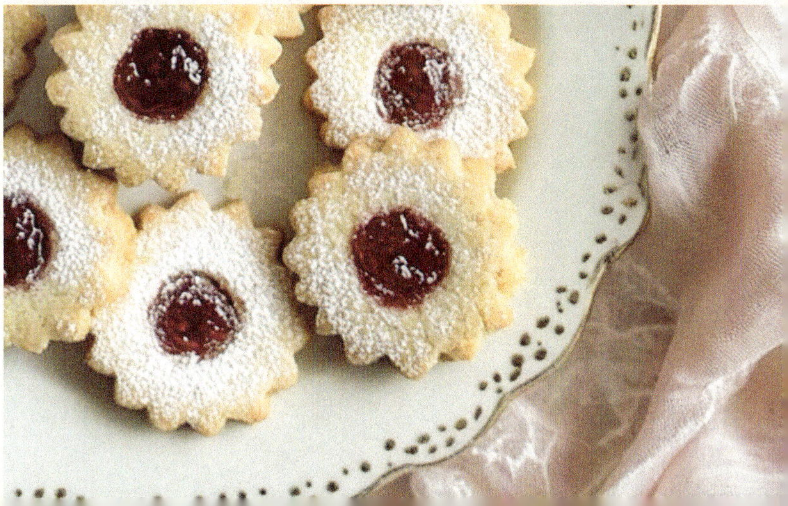

CLASSIC BUTTERY SHORTBREAD

Ingredients:

- 225 g unsalted butter, softened
- 90 g powdered sugar (icing sugar)
- 1 tsp pure vanilla extract
- 250 g all-purpose flour (plain flour)
- 65 g cornstarch (optional but recommended, for extra tenderness)
- ¼ tsp fine sea salt

Directions:

1. Preheat your oven to 325°F (160°C). Line two baking sheets with parchment paper.
2. In a large bowl, cream the butter and powdered sugar together using a hand mixer or stand mixer on medium speed, until light and fluffy (about 2-3 minutes).
3. Add the vanilla extract and mix briefly to combine.
4. Gradually add the flour, cornstarch, and salt, mixing on low speed until a soft dough forms. Scrape down the bowl as needed.
5. Transfer the dough to a lightly floured surface and gently knead it until smooth.
6. Roll out the dough to about ⅜ inch thick. Use a round cookie cutter (or your favorite shape) to cut out the cookies.
7. Place cookies on the prepared baking sheets, about 1 inch apart. If you like, you can prick the tops with a fork for a classic look.
8. Bake for 18-20 minutes, or until the edges are just barely golden (don't let them brown).
9. Cool on the baking sheets for 5 minutes, then transfer to a wire rack to cool completely.

Tips

For extra tenderness, don't overwork the dough. Handle it just enough to bring it together.

Dust with a little extra powdered sugar after baking for a beautiful, snowy finish.

Try dipping half of each cookie in melted chocolate and sprinkling with finely chopped nuts for a festive variation.

CLASSIC BUTTERY SHORTBREAD BISCUITS

Delicate, buttery, and melt-in-your-mouth perfection. These classic shortbread cookies are a timeless treat—simple yet elegant, with a hint of sweetness that makes them perfect for any occasion. Whether served at an afternoon tea or wrapped as a thoughtful gift, their light, crumbly texture and rich flavor never go out of style.

RASPBERRY WINDOW BISCUITS

Ingredients:

- 225 g unsalted butter, softened
- 90 g powdered sugar (icing sugar)
- 1 large egg yolk
- 1 tsp pure vanilla extract
- 280 g all-purpose flour (plain flour)
- 75 g almond flour (or finely ground blanched almonds)
- ¼ tsp fine sea salt
- 120 g raspberry jam (seedless, if preferred)
- Powdered sugar (icing sugar), for dusting

Directions:

1. Preheat your oven to 350°F (175°C). Line two baking sheets with parchment paper.
2. In a large bowl, cream together the butter and powdered sugar until light and fluffy.
3. Add the egg yolk and vanilla extract, and mix until combined.
4. In a separate bowl, whisk together the all-purpose flour, almond flour, and salt. Gradually add to the butter mixture, mixing until a soft dough forms.
5. Divide the dough in half. Flatten each portion into a disc, wrap in plastic, and chill for 30 minutes.
6. Roll out one disc of dough on a lightly floured surface to about ⅛ inch thick. Cut out cookies using a round cutter (about 2½ inches). For half the cookies, cut out a small window shape in the center (hearts, circles, stars work beautifully).
7. Transfer to baking sheets and bake for 10-12 minutes, or until lightly golden at the edges. Cool completely on a wire rack.
8. Spread raspberry jam on the flat side of each full cookie. Dust the windowed tops with powdered sugar, then place them gently on top of the jam to create a sandwich.

Tips

Chill the dough well to prevent spreading during baking.
Use a seedless jam for a smooth finish, or go for homemade for a rustic touch.
For an extra flourish, add a few edible flowers to your presentation.

RASPBERRY WINDOW BISCUITS

Beautiful inside and out, these delicate sandwich cookies reveal a jewel-like raspberry center through a dainty window. With their buttery texture and sweet jam filling, they're perfect for adding a little elegance to your cookie platter—or wrapping up as a thoughtful gift.

PRESSED FLOWER SHORTBREAD BISCUITS

Ingredients:

- 225g unsalted butter, softened
- 90g powdered sugar (¾ cup)
- 1 teaspoon pure vanilla extract
- 280g all-purpose flour (2¼ cups)
- 30g cornstarch (¼ cup)
- ¼ teaspoon fine sea salt
- ¼ cup edible flowers (pansies, violas, rose petals, lavender—ensure they are food-safe)
- 1 egg white (optional, for adhering the flowers)
- Granulated sugar, for sprinkling (optional)

Directions:

1. Preheat your oven to 325°F (160°C). Line two baking sheets with parchment paper.
2. In a large bowl, cream together the butter (225g) and powdered sugar (90g) until light and fluffy.
3. Add the vanilla extract and mix until just combined.
4. In a separate bowl, whisk together the all-purpose flour (280g), cornstarch (30g), and salt. Gradually add the dry ingredients to the butter mixture, mixing on low speed until a soft dough forms.
5. Divide the dough into two discs, wrap each in plastic wrap, and refrigerate for 30 minutes.
6. On a lightly floured surface, roll out one disc to about 6mm (¼ inch) thick. Cut into rounds or shapes of your choice.
7. Place the cookies on the prepared baking sheets.
8. Gently press an edible flower onto the center of each cookie. Brush lightly with egg white, if using, to help the flower adhere and give a gentle sheen.
9. Optionally, sprinkle with a little granulated sugar for a subtle sparkle.
10. Bake for 12-15 minutes, until just pale golden at the edges. Do not let them brown.
11. Cool on the tray for 5 minutes before transferring to a wire rack to cool completely.

Tips

Use room temperature butter for easy creaming and a smooth dough.

Choose flat, small edible flowers for the best visual effect.

These cookies store well in an airtight container for up to 5 days.

PRESSED FLOWER SHORTBREAD BISCUITS

Delicate and elegant, these buttery shortbread cookies are adorned with edible flowers for a stunning, natural finish. Perfect for afternoon teas, weddings, or as a thoughtful gift, they're almost too beautiful to eat.

PISTACHIO ROSEWATER THUMBPRINT BISCUITS

Ingredients:

- 225g unsalted butter, softened

- 100g powdered sugar (¾ cup)

- 1 teaspoon pure vanilla extract

- ½ teaspoon rosewater (adjust to taste)

- 280g all-purpose flour (2¼ cups)

- ¼ teaspoon fine sea salt

- 60g finely ground pistachios (½ cup)

- 6 tablespoons raspberry or rose petal jam

- 2 tablespoons chopped pistachios (for garnish, optional)

- Powdered sugar, for dusting (optional)

Directions:

1. Preheat your oven to 325°F (160°C). Line two baking sheets with parchment paper.
2. In a large bowl, cream together the butter (225g) and powdered sugar (100g) until light and fluffy.
3. Add the vanilla extract and rosewater, mixing gently until combined.
4. In a separate bowl, whisk together the all-purpose flour (280g), ground pistachios (60g), and salt.
5. Gradually add the dry ingredients to the butter mixture and mix until a soft dough forms.
6. Scoop tablespoon-sized portions of dough and roll into balls. Place them 2 inches apart on the prepared baking sheets.
7. Use your thumb or the back of a small spoon to make an indentation in the center of each cookie.
8. Bake for 12-14 minutes, until just set and lightly golden at the edges.
9. Remove from the oven and, if the indentations have puffed, gently press them again while warm. Cool completely on a wire rack.
10. Once cooled, spoon a small amount of raspberry or rose petal jam into each indentation.
11. Garnish with chopped pistachios and a light dusting of powdered sugar, if desired.

Tips

Use high-quality rosewater for a delicate, fragrant flavor—not overpowering.
Choose pale green pistachios (unsalted) for the most elegant look.
Fill with rose petal jam for an exotic twist, or classic raspberry for a pop of color.

PISTACHIO ROSEWATER THUMBPRINT BISCUITS

Fragrant with rosewater and adorned with jewel-like centers, these pistachio thumbprint cookies make an elegant and thoughtful gift. Beautifully delicate and easy to prepare, they're a luxurious twist on a classic favorite.

CHOCOLATE-DIPPED HAZELNUT BISCOTTI

Ingredients:

- 115g unsalted butter, softened

- 150g granulated sugar (¾ cup)

- 2 large eggs

- 1 teaspoon pure vanilla extract

- 280g all-purpose flour (2¼ cups)

- 1½ teaspoons baking powder

- ¼ teaspoon fine sea salt

- 120g chopped toasted hazelnuts (1 cup)

- 200g dark chocolate (for dipping)

- 2 tablespoons finely chopped hazelnuts (for garnish, optional)

Directions:

1. Preheat your oven to 350°F (175°C). Line a baking sheet with parchment paper.
2. In a large bowl, cream together the butter (115g) and sugar (150g) until light and fluffy.
3. Add the eggs, one at a time, mixing well after each addition. Stir in the vanilla extract.
4. In a separate bowl, whisk together the flour (280g), baking powder, and salt. Gradually add to the wet ingredients until combined.
5. Stir in the chopped hazelnuts (120g).
6. Divide the dough in half and shape each into a log about 12 inches long and 2 inches wide. Place both logs on the prepared baking sheet, spacing them apart.
7. Bake for 25–30 minutes, until lightly golden and set. Remove from the oven and allow to cool for 10 minutes.
8. Using a serrated knife, slice the logs diagonally into ½ inch thick slices.
9. Arrange the slices cut-side down on the baking sheet and return to the oven. Bake for another 10 minutes, flip, then bake an additional 10 minutes until dry and crisp.
10. Once cooled, dip one end of each biscotti in melted dark chocolate. Place on parchment paper and sprinkle with chopped hazelnuts before the chocolate sets.

Tips

- Toast the hazelnuts beforehand for maximum flavor.
- Use a good quality dark chocolate (at least 60% cocoa) for dipping.
- Biscotti can be stored in an airtight container for up to two weeks—perfect for gifting!

CHOCOLATE-DIPPED HAZELNUT BISCOTTI

Delicately crunchy and infused with the rich, nutty flavour of roasted hazelnuts, these chocolate-dipped biscotti are an elegant twist on a classic Italian favourite. Each crisp slice is dipped in smooth, dark chocolate and finished with a sprinkle of finely chopped hazelnuts, making them as beautiful to present as they are delicious to enjoy. Perfect alongside a cup of espresso or as part of a thoughtful homemade gift, these biscotti are easy to make, store well, and never fail to impress.

VANILLA SABLÉS

Ingredients:

- 225g unsalted butter, softened
- 100g powdered sugar (¾ cup)
- 2 teaspoons pure vanilla extract (or vanilla bean paste for extra elegance)
- 280g all-purpose flour (2¼ cups)
- ¼ teaspoon fine sea salt
- 1 egg yolk (for brushing)
- 2 tablespoons demerara or turbinado sugar (for rolling)

Directions:

1. In a large mixing bowl, cream together the butter (225g) and powdered sugar (100g) until pale and fluffy.
2. Add the vanilla extract (or vanilla bean paste) and mix briefly to combine.
3. In a separate bowl, whisk together the flour (280g) and salt.
4. Gradually add the dry ingredients to the butter mixture and mix until a soft dough forms.
5. Divide the dough into two portions and shape each into a log, about 2 inches (5 cm) in diameter.
6. Wrap each log in parchment paper or plastic wrap and chill for at least 1 hour (or overnight for deeper flavour).
7. Preheat the oven to 325°F (160°C). Line two baking sheets with parchment paper.
8. Unwrap the logs and brush lightly with egg yolk. Roll each log in demerara or turbinado sugar to create a sparkling edge.
9. Slice into ¼ inch (6mm) thick rounds and place on the prepared baking sheets, leaving space between them.
10. Bake for 12-15 minutes, or until the edges are just beginning to turn golden.
11. Cool on the baking sheet for 5 minutes, then transfer to a wire rack to cool completely

Tips

- Vanilla bean paste gives a luxurious flavour and those beautiful specks of vanilla throughout the cookies.
- The sugar-crusted edges add a lovely crunch and sparkle—perfect for a refined presentation.

VANILLA SABLÉS

Elegant in their simplicity, these classic French butter cookies are infused with vanilla and finished with a sparkling sugar edge. Their delicate texture and rich flavour make them a timeless addition to any cookie collection, perfect for both everyday enjoyment and special occasions.

ITALIAN AMARETTI BISCUITS

Ingredients:

- 200g almond flour (finely ground blanched almonds)
- 150g granulated sugar (¾ cup)
- 2 large egg whites
- ½ teaspoon pure almond extract
- ½ teaspoon pure vanilla extract
- ¼ teaspoon fine sea salt
- Powdered sugar, for dusting (about 50g / ½ cup)

Directions:

1. Preheat the oven to 325°F (160°C). Line two baking sheets with parchment paper.
2. In a medium bowl, whisk together the almond flour (200g) and granulated sugar (150g) until combined.
3. In a separate bowl, beat the egg whites with a pinch of salt until soft peaks form.
4. Gently fold the egg whites into the almond flour mixture until a soft, sticky dough forms.
5. Add the almond extract and vanilla extract, mixing just until incorporated.
6. With lightly dampened hands, roll heaping teaspoons of dough into small balls (about 1 inch / 2.5 cm in diameter).
7. Roll each ball in powdered sugar to coat thoroughly.
8. Place the cookies on the prepared baking sheets, spacing them about 2 inches apart.
9. Bake for 20–25 minutes, or until the cookies are lightly golden on the outside and soft inside.
10. Allow to cool on the baking sheet for 5 minutes before transferring to a wire rack to cool completely.

Baker's Tips

1. Use good quality almond flour for the best flavor and texture.
2. The egg whites should be just softly beaten, not stiff peaks.
3. Store in an airtight container for up to a week, or freeze for longer storage.

ITALIAN AMARETTI BISCUITS

With their delicate almond flavor and lightly crisp exterior, these Italian Amaretti cookies are a timeless favorite. Dusted in powdered sugar and naturally gluten-free, they make a beautiful addition to any platter or gift box.

LAVENDER SHORTBREAD HEARTS

Ingredients:

- 225g unsalted butter, softened
- 90g powdered sugar (¾ cup)
- 2 teaspoons dried culinary lavender buds (finely chopped)
- 1 teaspoon pure vanilla extract
- 280g all-purpose flour (2¼ cups)
- 30g cornstarch (¼ cup)
- ¼ teaspoon fine sea salt
- Extra granulated sugar or edible glitter, for sprinkling (optional)

Directions:

1. Preheat your oven to 325°F (160°C). Line two baking sheets with parchment paper.
2. In a large bowl, cream together the softened butter (225g) and powdered sugar (90g) until pale and fluffy.
3. Add the vanilla extract and finely chopped lavender buds, mixing gently to combine.
4. In a separate bowl, whisk together the flour (280g), cornstarch (30g), and salt.
5. Gradually add the dry ingredients to the butter mixture and mix on low speed until a soft dough forms.
6. Divide the dough into two portions, flatten each into a disc, wrap in plastic wrap, and refrigerate for 30 minutes.
7. On a lightly floured surface, roll out the dough to about 6mm (¼ inch) thick.
8. Cut out heart shapes with a cookie cutter and place on the prepared baking sheets, spacing them slightly apart.
9. Sprinkle with granulated sugar or a dusting of edible glitter, if desired.
10. Bake for 12-15 minutes, or until the edges are just beginning to turn pale golden.
11. Allow to cool on the baking sheet for 5 minutes before transferring to a wire rack to cool completely.
12. Baker's Tips
13. Use culinary-grade lavender only (never ornamental varieties).
14. Chop the lavender finely for a subtle, even flavor throughout the cookie.
15. Package in clear cellophane bags tied with blush ribbon or in gift boxes lined with tissue paper for an elegant presentation

LAVENDER SHORTBREAD HEARTS

Fragrant with delicate lavender and shaped into charming hearts, these buttery shortbread biscuits are as beautiful as they are delicious. Whether wrapped as an elegant gift or served at a garden tea party, they add grace and refinement to any occasion.

DECORATED COOKIES & BISCUITS

Some biscuits are almost too beautiful to eat—almost. This chapter is a celebration of decorating, where each biscuit becomes a miniature canvas and every design tells a story. These recipes are an invitation to slow down, savour the details, and create something truly special.

Whether you're delicately piping royal icing, pressing elegant stamps into buttery dough, or cutting festive shapes for a celebration, these biscuits are designed to impress long before the first bite.

Decorated biscuits have a way of transforming simple moments into lasting memories. They grace wedding dessert tables, add sparkle to holiday gatherings, and make thoughtful edible gifts tied with ribbon. They can be as refined as lace-detailed sugar biscuits or as playful as whimsical shapes for children's parties—each one carrying a personal touch that makes it unforgettable.

In this chapter, you'll find a collection of elegant recipes that celebrate both beauty and flavour. With step-by-step guidance for achieving smooth royal icing finishes, tips for piping intricate patterns, and ideas for adding texture through stamps and embossers, these recipes will inspire you to decorate with confidence and creativity. Whether you're an experienced biscuit decorator or just beginning, you'll find something here to spark your imagination—and delight your taste buds.

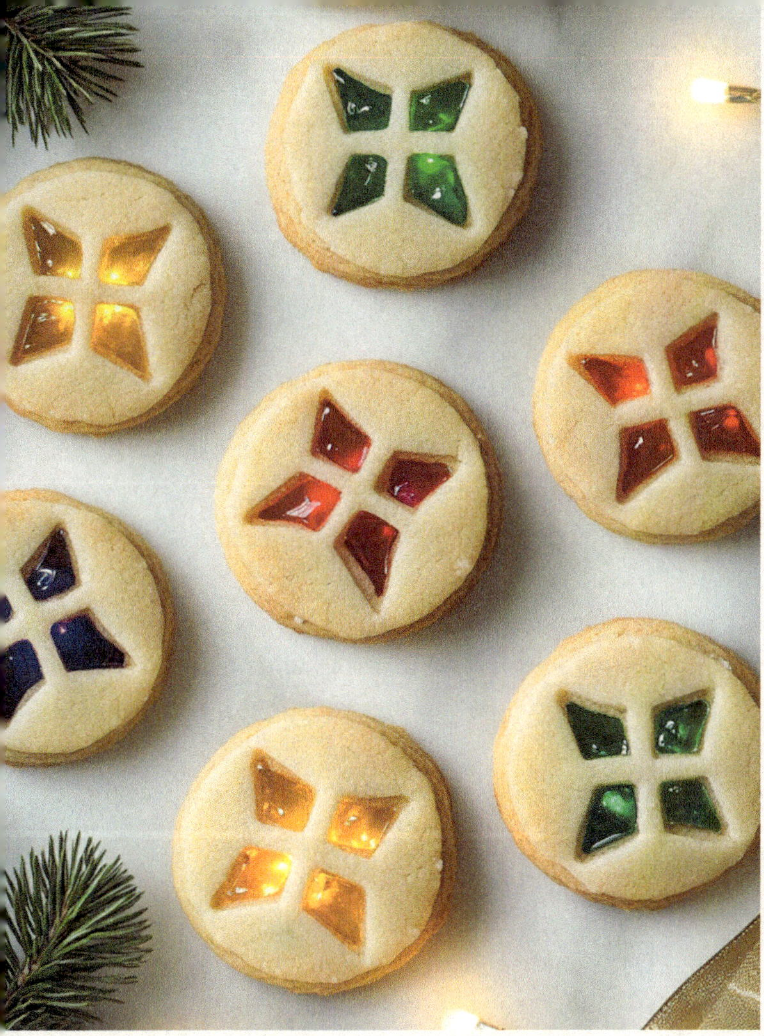
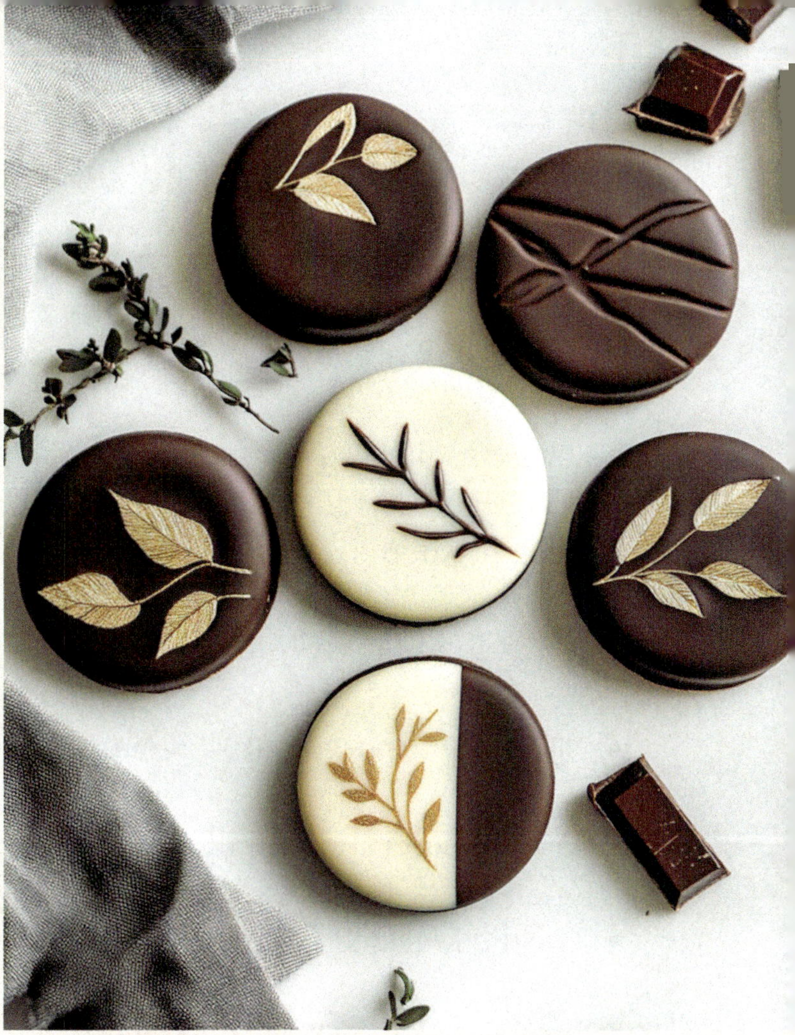
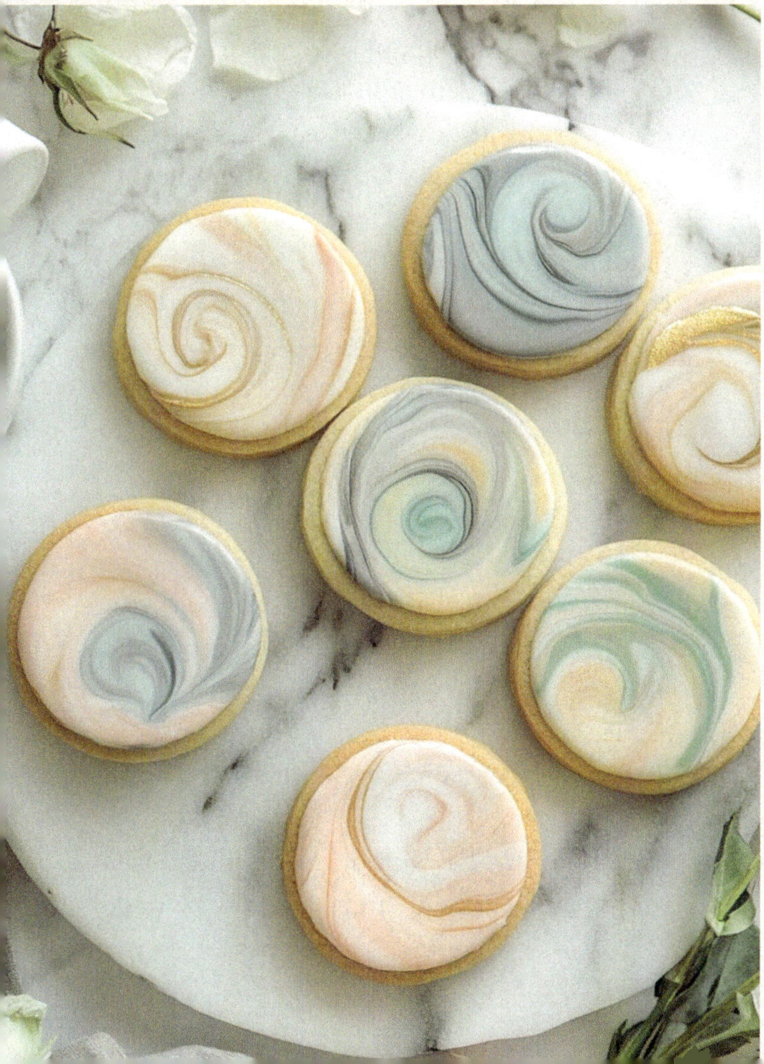
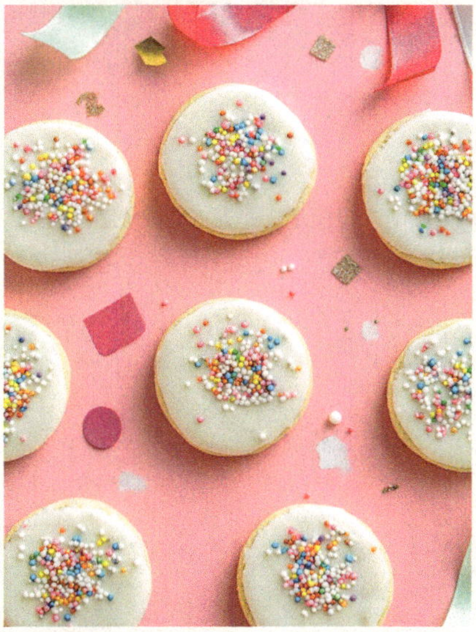
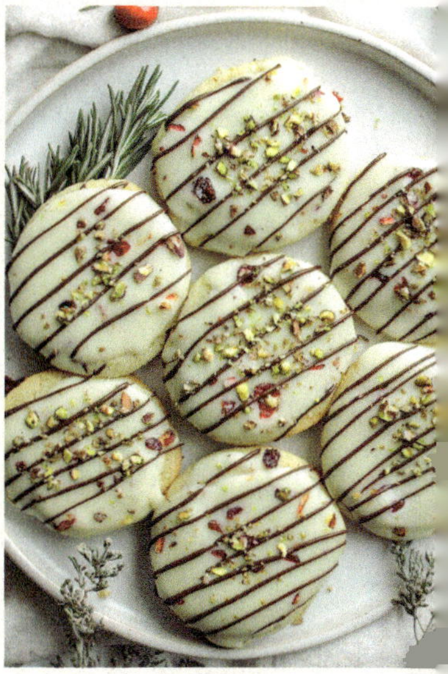
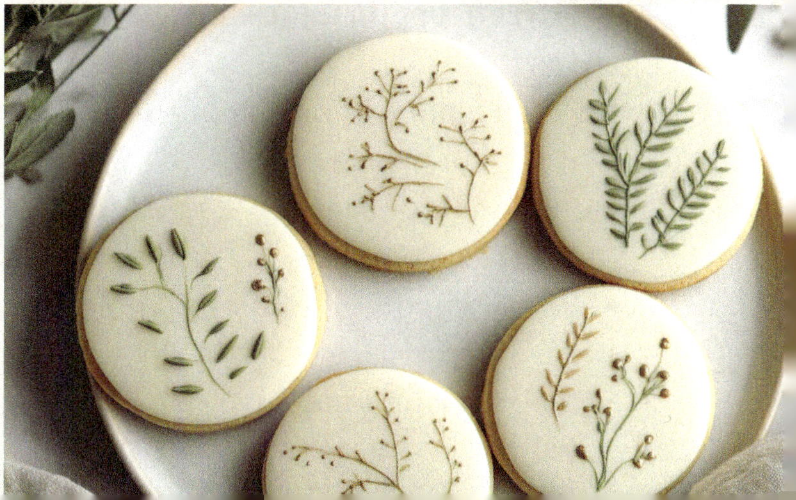

MARBLED FONDANT GLAZE BISCUITS

Ingredients:

- 225g unsalted butter, softened
- 100g powdered sugar (¾ cup)
- 1 teaspoon pure vanilla extract
- 280g all-purpose flour (2¼ cups)
- ¼ teaspoon fine sea salt
- For the Marbled Fondant Glaze:
- 250g ready-to-roll white fondant
- Gel food coloring in 2-3 complementary colors (e.g., blush, ivory, pale grey, or jewel tones)
- Cornstarch, for dusting
- Clear alcohol (vodka or lemon extract), optional for shine
- Edible gold leaf or metallic food paint (optional for accents)
- Small amount of water or edible glue for adhering fondant

Directions:

1. For the Biscuits
2. In a large bowl, cream together the butter (225g) and powdered sugar (100g) until smooth and fluffy.
3. Add vanilla extract and mix briefly to combine.
4. Sift together the flour (280g) and salt. Add gradually to the butter mixture until a soft dough forms.
5. Turn the dough onto a floured surface and roll out to 6mm (¼ inch) thickness.
6. Cut out shapes using round or geometric cookie cutters for a modern look.
7. Place cookies on parchment-lined trays and chill for 15 minutes before baking.
8. Bake at 325°F (160°C) for 12-15 minutes, until pale golden. Cool completely before decorating.
9. For the Marbled Fondant Glaze:
10. Lightly dust your work surface with cornstarch. Roll out the white fondant to 2-3mm thick.
11. Add small drops of gel food coloring onto the fondant surface (use gloves if needed).
12. Fold and twist the fondant gently, then roll it out again to create marbled swirls—don't over-mix, or the colors will blend too much.
13. Use the same cookie cutter to cut out fondant shapes matching your cookies.
14. Brush a thin layer of water or edible glue on top of each cookie.

Gently press the marbled fondant onto the cookie, smoothing lightly with your hands or a fondant smoother.

Baker's Tips

- Stick to 2-3 colors for an elegant marbled effect; less is more.
- Jewel tones work beautifully for evening events, while pastels feel airy and romantic for weddings.

MARBLED FONDANT GLAZE BISCUITS

These marbled fondant glaze cookies are as striking as they are simple to create. Each cookie is topped with a one-of-a-kind swirl of smooth fondant, mimicking the look of marbled stone or delicate watercolor artwork. Choose soft pastels—like blush pink, ivory, and pale grey—for an airy, romantic finish perfect for weddings and afternoon teas, or opt for deep jewel tones such as emerald green, sapphire blue, and rich burgundy to create a dramatic, luxurious effect ideal for evening events and modern celebrations.

CHOCOLATE TRANSFER BISCUITS

Ingredients:

- For the Biscuits
- 225g unsalted butter, softened
- 100g powdered sugar (¾ cup)
- 1 teaspoon vanilla extract
- 280g all-purpose flour (2¼ cups)
- ¼ teaspoon fine sea salt
- For the Chocolate Topping:
- 200g chocolate melts or compound chocolate (dark, milk, or white)
- Chocolate transfer sheets (cut to size)

Directions:

1. For the Biscuits
2. Cream together the butter (225g) and powdered sugar (100g) until fluffy.
3. Add the vanilla extract and mix well.
4. Stir in the flour (280g) and salt until a soft dough forms.
5. Roll out to 6mm (¼ inch) thick, cut into rounds or rectangles, and chill for 10-15 minutes.
6. Bake at 325°F (160°C) for 12-15 minutes until lightly golden. Cool completely.
7. For the Topping (Easy Method!)
8. Melt the chocolate melts according to package directions (no tempering needed!).
9. Spread a thin layer of melted chocolate onto the cooled cookies using an offset spatula.
10. While the chocolate is still wet, press a cut piece of chocolate transfer sheet (design side down) onto the chocolate.
11. Let it sit at room temperature until set (about 20-30 minutes).
12. Peel off the backing to reveal your beautiful design!
13. Optional Simple Variation
14. Use chocolate discs with printed designs and attach to your cookies with a dab of icing or chocolate.
15. Or, pipe a circle of melted chocolate on top of each cookie and press the disc into place.

Baker's Tips (For Beginners!):
- Chocolate melts don't need tempering and are perfect for beginner-friendly decorating.
- Pre-cut the transfer sheets while your cookies are baking.
- Work on small batches to keep the process smooth and stress-free!

CHOCOLATE TRANSFER BISCUITS

These chocolate transfer cookies make it simple to create polished, professional-looking treats—no advanced skills required! With sleek, modern designs pressed into smooth chocolate, they're perfect for weddings, elegant gifts, or adding a sophisticated touch to your cookie tray.

STAINED GLASS BISCUITS

Ingredients:

- For the Biscuits
- 225g unsalted butter, softened
- 150g granulated sugar (¾ cup)
- 1 large egg
- 1½ teaspoons pure vanilla extract
- 300g all-purpose flour (2½ cups)
- ½ teaspoon baking powder
- ¼ teaspoon fine sea salt
- For the Stained Glass Filling:
- 150g clear hard candies (like Jolly Ranchers or Lifesavers), separated by color
- Optional: Edible gold dust for edges (for an elegant touch)
- Optional: Ribbon or twine if making them into hanging cookies

Directions:

1. Make the Biscuits Dough:
2. Cream the butter (225g) and sugar (150g) until pale and fluffy.
3. Beat in the egg and vanilla extract.
4. In a separate bowl, whisk together the flour (300g), baking powder (½ tsp), and salt (¼ tsp).
5. Gradually add the dry ingredients to the wet mixture until a dough forms.
6. Divide the dough into two discs, wrap, and chill for at least 30 minutes.
7. Roll, Cut, and Shape:
8. Preheat the oven to 350°F (175°C). Line baking sheets with parchment paper.
9. Roll the dough out to about ¼ inch (6mm) thick.
10. Cut out large shapes (stars, hearts, circles).
11. Use a smaller cutter to cut out the center, creating a window.
12. Place the cookies on the prepared sheets.
13. Crush the candies by color (in a bag with a rolling pin or in a food processor).
14. Fill and Bake:
15. Spoon the crushed candy into the cut-out centers.
16. Bake for 8–10 minutes, until the cookies are lightly golden and the candy has melted.
17. Cool completely on the baking sheet before moving.
18. Optional: Dust the edges of the cookies lightly with edible gold dust for an elegant finish.
19. Optional Hanging Version:
20. Before baking, use a straw to poke a hole at the top of each cookie for threading ribbon.

Tips for Success
- Make sure the candy melts completely flat before removing from the oven.
- Use clear candies for a glass-like effect (avoid opaque candies).

STAINED GLASS COOKIES

Light catches the jewel-toned centers of these beautiful stained glass cookies, making them as much decoration as dessert. Whether hung from a Christmas tree, gifted in clear boxes, or served at a party, these cookies add a little sparkle and fun to your baking.

PAINTED BOTANICAL FONDANT BISCUITS

Ingredients:

- For the Sugar Cookies:
- 225g unsalted butter, softened
- 100g powdered sugar (¾ cup)
- 1 large egg
- 1 tsp vanilla extract
- 300g all-purpose flour (2½ cups)
- ¼ tsp fine sea salt
- For the Decorations:
- 250g ready-to-roll fondant (white or pale pastel)
- Edible food coloring pens (green, brown, pink, etc.)
- Optional: Edible gold paint or gold leaf for accents
- Edible glue or water
- Cornstarch (for rolling out fondant)

Directions:

1. Step 1: Make the Biscuits
2. In a large bowl, beat butter and powdered sugar until smooth (about 1-2 minutes).
3. Add the egg and vanilla. Mix until combined.
4. Stir in flour and salt until a soft dough forms.
5. Shape dough into a disc, wrap in plastic, and chill for 30 minutes.
6. Preheat oven to 350°F (175°C).
7. Roll out dough on a floured surface to ¼ inch (6mm) thick. Cut into rounds or other simple shapes.
8. Place on lined trays and chill for 10 minutes.
9. Bake for 10-12 minutes until lightly golden. Cool completely.
10. Step 2: Add the Fondant
11. Dust your work surface with cornstarch. Roll out fondant to about 2mm thick.
12. Cut out fondant using the same cookie cutter as the cookies.
13. Brush a little water or edible glue on top of each cookie.
14. Gently press fondant onto each cookie and smooth with your fingers.
15. Step 3: Decorate with Edible Pens
16. Use edible food coloring pens to draw simple botanical designs directly onto the fondant.
17. Try vines, leaves, or tiny flowers—stick to one or two colors for a minimalist look.
18. Optional: Add dots of edible gold paint or flecks of edible gold leaf for a luxury finish.

Baker's Tips
- Keep designs simple! Even dots or dashes can look chic.
- Use fine-tipped edible pens for best results.
- Let fondant dry for 15 minutes before drawing for smoother lines.

PAINTED BOTANICAL FONDANT BISCUITS

These elegant sugar cookies are topped with smooth fondant and hand-painted with delicate botanical designs. Whether you're a beginner or experienced baker, you'll find these surprisingly simple and utterly impressive. They're perfect for weddings, garden parties, or luxury gifting.

CONFETTI DIPPED BISCUITS

Ingredients:

- For the Biscuits
- 225g unsalted butter, softened
- 100g powdered sugar (¾ cup)
- 1 tsp vanilla extract
- 300g all-purpose flour (2½ cups)
- ¼ tsp fine sea salt
- For the Decoration
- 200g chocolate melts (white, milk, or dark)
- Assorted sprinkles or confetti (rainbow, pastel, or metallic)

Directions:

Step 1: Make the Biscuits
1. Cream butter and powdered sugar until smooth.
2. Add vanilla extract.
3. Stir in flour and salt until a soft dough forms.
4. Roll dough to 6mm (¼ inch) and cut into circles, stars, or hearts.
5. Chill cut cookies for 10 minutes.
6. Bake at 350°F (175°C) for 10–12 minutes until lightly golden. Cool completely.
7. Step 2: Dip and Decorate
8. Melt chocolate melts according to package directions.
9. Dip half of each cookie into the chocolate, letting excess drip off.
10. Immediately sprinkle confetti or sprinkles over the wet chocolate.
11. Place on parchment paper and allow chocolate to set at room temperature (about 30 minutes).
12. Baker's Tips
13. Use pastel sprinkles for a soft, elegant look, or metallic confetti for modern sophistication.
14. Melted candy melts set faster than real chocolate—great for beginners!
15. Package in clear cellophane bags for gifting.

CONFETTI DIPPED BISCUITS

Bring a pop of colour and joy to your biscuit collection with these delightful Confetti-Dipped biscuits. Simple, fun, and endlessly versatile, these buttery treats are half-dipped in smooth chocolate and generously coated in playful sprinkles or shimmering confetti. Whether you go for bold rainbow hues, pastel palettes, or chic metallics, each becomes a celebration all on its own.

WHITE CHOCOLATE DRIZZLE & DRIED FRUIT BISCUITS

Ingredients:

- For the Biscuits

- 225g unsalted butter, softened

- 100g powdered sugar (¾ cup)

- 1 tsp vanilla extract

- 300g all-purpose flour (2½ cups)

- ¼ tsp fine sea salt

- For the Topping

- 150g white chocolate melts

- 50g finely chopped dried cranberries, apricots, pistachios, or a combination

- Optional: Edible gold flakes or shimmer dust

Directions:

Step 1: Make the Biscuits
1. Cream butter and powdered sugar until smooth and fluffy.
2. Add vanilla extract and mix well.
3. Stir in flour and salt until a soft dough forms.
4. Roll out dough to 6mm (¼ inch) and cut into rounds, ovals, or rectangles for a modern look.
5. Chill cut cookies for 10 minutes.
6. Bake at 350°F (175°C) for 10–12 minutes, until edges are pale golden. Cool completely.
7. Step 2: Decorate
8. Melt white chocolate melts in the microwave or over a double boiler until smooth.
9. Using a spoon or piping bag, drizzle white chocolate over the cooled cookies in a zig-zag pattern.
10. Immediately sprinkle chopped dried fruit and nuts over the wet chocolate.
11. Optional: Add a pinch of edible gold flakes or shimmer dust for an elegant finish.
12. Let set at room temperature for 30 minutes before serving or packaging.
13. Baker's Tips
14. For a more refined look, stick to one or two dried fruits and matching colour palettes (e.g., cranberries and pistachios for a festive feel).
15. You can use dark or milk chocolate instead of white for a different look.

WHITE CHOCOLATE DRIZZLE & DRIED FRUIT BISCUITS

These biscuits are a no-fuss, yet elegant option, perfect for when you want to add a sophisticated touch without complicated techniques. A buttery biscuit base is finished with a generous drizzle of creamy white chocolate and a sprinkle of dried fruits like cranberries, apricots, or pistachios for texture, colour, and flavour. Think minimal effort, maximum elegance.

FESTIVE & SEASONAL FAVORITES

There's something magical about baking with the seasons—celebrating life's special moments with something sweet from the oven. In this collection of Festive & Seasonal Favourites, you'll find biscuits that mark every occasion—whether it's the comforting warmth of spiced gingerbread at Christmas, delicate lemon biscuits at Easter, or showstopping designs for birthdays and celebrations.

These recipes are made to bring joy and beauty to your holiday tables, party platters, and edible gifts. Many are wonderfully simple, offering options for both beginners and experienced bakers who want to create something special without the stress. Each biscuit is crafted to be as visually charming as it is delicious, blending tradition, celebration, and a little everyday magic in every bite.

From cosy, nostalgic classics to playful, modern designs, these biscuits capture the spirit of the seasons and help make every occasion just a little more magical.

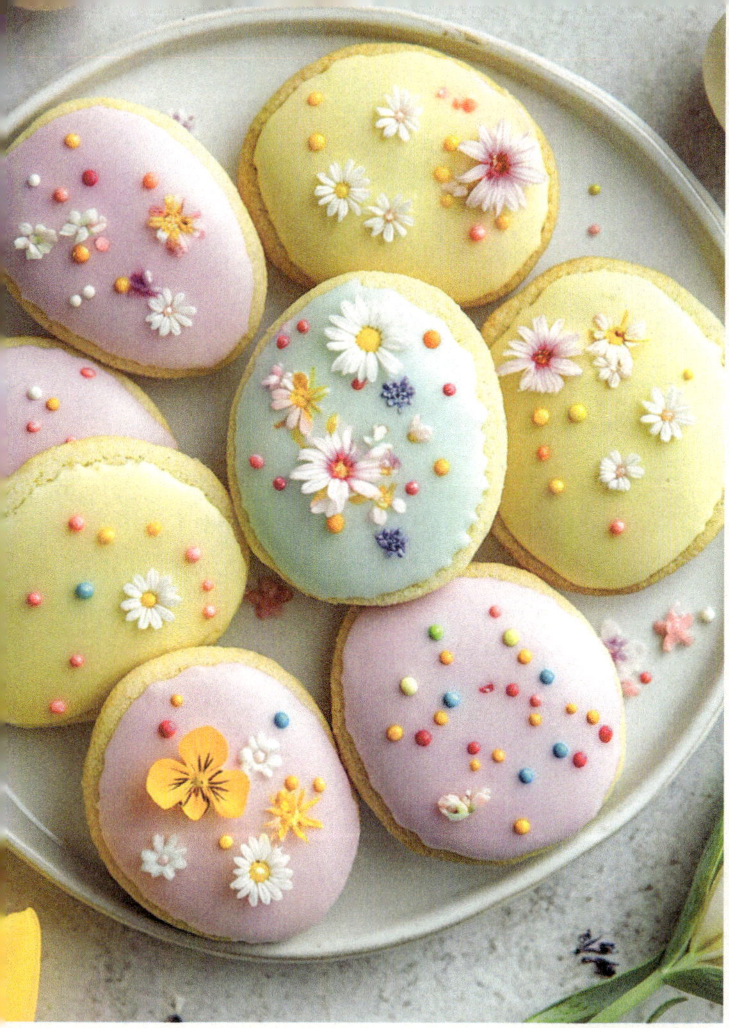
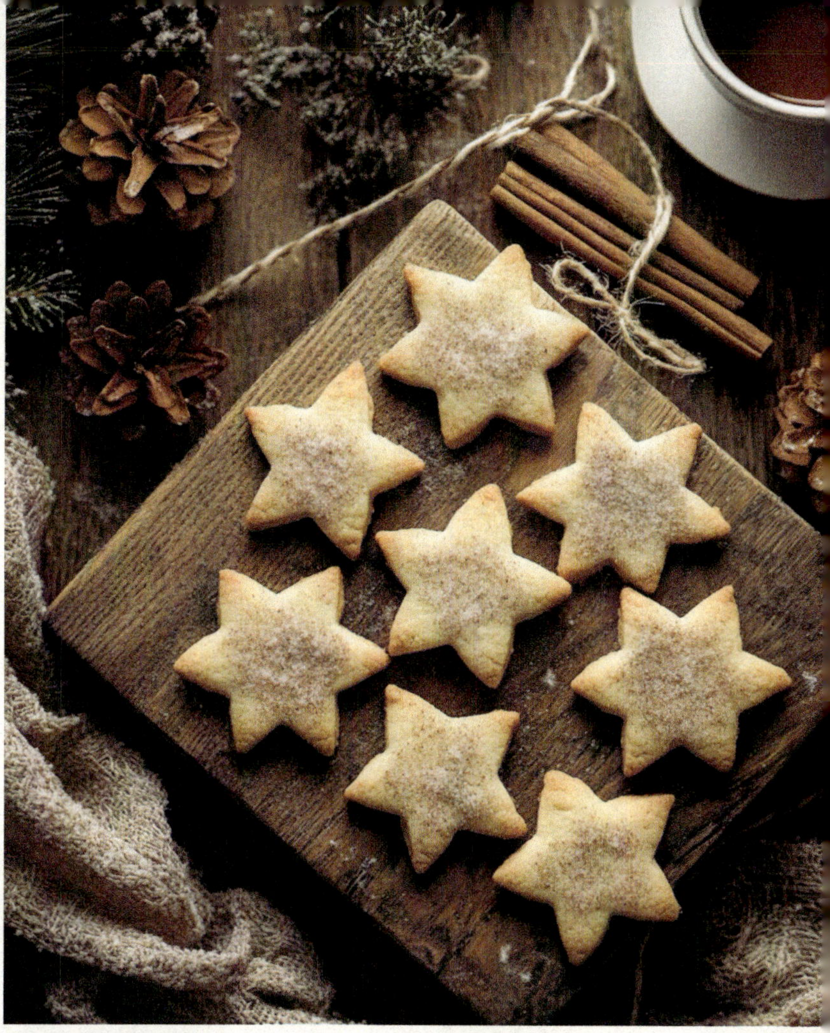
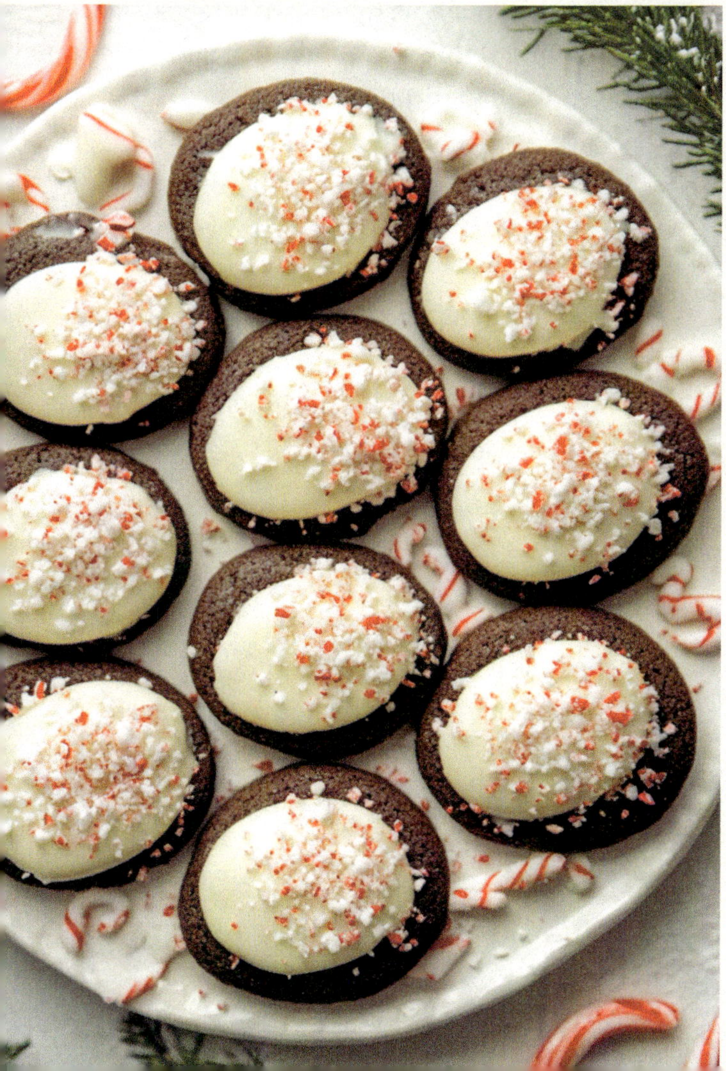
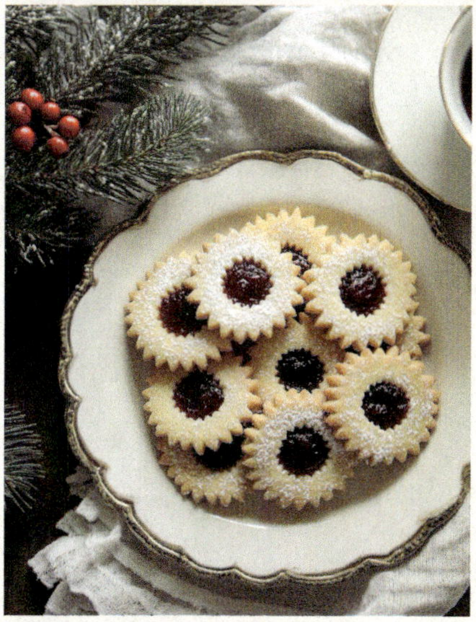
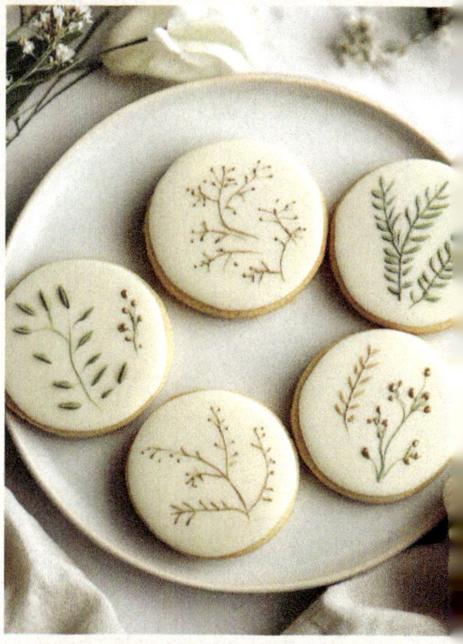
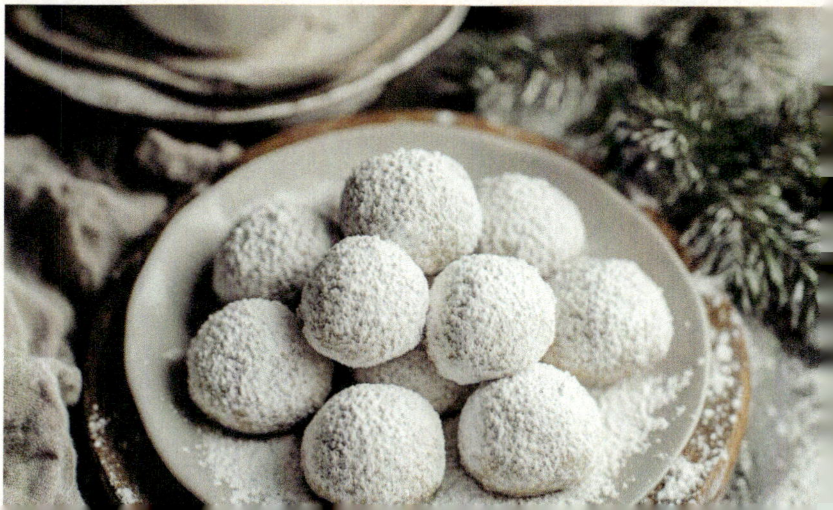

SPICED GINGERBREAD STARS

Ingredients:

- 150g unsalted butter, softened
- 100g light brown sugar (½ cup, packed)
- 120g molasses (⅓ cup)
- 1 large egg
- 350g all-purpose flour (2¾ cups)
- 1½ teaspoons ground ginger
- 1 teaspoon ground cinnamon
- ½ teaspoon ground nutmeg
- ¼ teaspoon ground cloves
- ½ teaspoon baking soda
- ¼ teaspoon fine sea salt

For Decorating:

- Royal icing (homemade or store-bought)
- Edible gold or silver pearls

Directions:

1. In a large bowl, cream together the butter (150g) and brown sugar (100g) until light and fluffy.
2. Add the molasses (120g) and egg, and beat until well combined.
3. In a separate bowl, sift together the flour (350g), ginger, cinnamon, nutmeg, cloves, baking soda, and salt.
4. Gradually add the dry ingredients to the wet, mixing on low speed until a soft dough forms.
5. Divide the dough into two discs, wrap in plastic wrap, and chill for at least 1 hour.
6. Preheat the oven to 350°F (175°C). Line baking sheets with parchment paper.
7. Roll out the dough on a lightly floured surface to ¼ inch (6mm) thickness. Cut into star shapes (or any festive shapes you like).
8. Transfer to baking sheets and bake for 8–10 minutes, until just set. Let cool on the tray for 5 minutes before transferring to a wire rack to cool completely.
9. Once cooled, decorate with royal icing—simple outlines, snowflakes, or intricate lace patterns. Sprinkle with sanding sugar or add edible pearls for extra elegance.

Tips

- Chill the dough well to prevent spreading and ensure crisp edges.
- Use piping bags with fine tips for delicate icing designs.
- These cookies store beautifully and can be made ahead—ideal for gifting!

SPICED GINGERBREAD STARS

Warmly spiced and delicately decorated, these gingerbread stars bring a touch of elegance to festive baking. With their crisp edges and soft interiors, they're perfect for holiday gatherings or wrapped as beautiful homemade gifts.

If piping isn't your style, you can use store-bought royal icing pens or ready-to-use icing tubes available in most grocery stores or baking supply shops.

CINNAMON SUGAR STARS

Ingredients:

- 225g unsalted butter, softened
- 100g powdered sugar (¾ cup)
- 1 tsp vanilla extract
- 300g all-purpose flour (2½ cups)
- ¼ tsp fine sea salt
- 50g granulated sugar (¼ cup)
- 1 tbsp ground cinnamon

Directions:

Step 1: Make the Biscuits

1. Cream the butter and powdered sugar until light and fluffy.
2. Add the vanilla extract and mix well.
3. Stir in flour and salt until a soft dough forms.
4. Roll dough to 6mm (¼ inch) thick and cut out star shapes.
5. Chill cut-outs for 10 minutes.
6. Preheat oven to 350°F (175°C).
7. Bake cookies for 10–12 minutes until the edges are just golden.
8. Cool slightly on the tray.
9. Step 2: Dust with Cinnamon Sugar
10. Mix granulated sugar and cinnamon in a small bowl.
11. While cookies are still warm, brush lightly with melted butter (optional for extra flavor) and sprinkle generously with the cinnamon sugar mixture.
12. Let cool completely.

Tips

- Chill the dough before cutting to keep the star shapes crisp and clean.
- Brush cookies with a little melted butter before sprinkling cinnamon sugar for extra flavor and for the sugar to stick better.
- Use fine cinnamon for a smoother coating and better balance with the sugar.
- Bake a little longer for a crisper cookie, perfect for dunking in tea or hot chocolate.

CINNAMON SUGAR STARS

Simple, timeless, and full of nostalgic charm, these Cinnamon Sugar Stars are a celebration of simplicity done right. Buttery and tender, with a subtle sweetness, they're baked to a light golden finish and coated in a fragrant blend of cinnamon and sugar. Perfect for sharing during the holiday season or serving alongside a cosy cup of tea, these stars are as beautiful on a platter as they are delightful to eat. Whether you gift them or keep them for your own festive table, these biscuits bring comfort and joy in every bite.

CHOCOLATE PEPPERMINT DIPPED BISCUITS

Ingredients:

- For the Biscuits
- 225g unsalted butter, softened
- 150g granulated sugar (¾ cup)
- 1 large egg
- 1 tsp vanilla extract
- 200g all-purpose flour (1½ cups)
- 60g cocoa powder (½ cup)
- ½ tsp baking soda
- ¼ tsp fine sea salt
- For the Decoration
- 150g white chocolate melts
- 4-5 peppermint candy canes, crushed finely

Directions:

1. Make the Biscuits
2. Cream butter and sugar until smooth and fluffy.
3. Add egg and vanilla, mixing well.
4. In a separate bowl, whisk together flour, cocoa, baking soda, and salt.
5. Gradually add dry ingredients to the wet until a dough forms.
6. Roll into balls, flatten slightly, or cut out rounds for a clean edge.
7. Bake at 350°F (175°C) for 10-12 minutes. Cool completely.
8. Step 2: Dip and Decorate
9. Melt white chocolate according to package instructions.
10. Dip half of each cookie into the white chocolate.
11. Immediately sprinkle crushed peppermint over the wet chocolate.

Place on parchment and let set at room temperature.

Tips

- Crush candy canes into small pieces, but not powder—they should have a little crunch and visual appeal.
- Use candy melts for the white chocolate if you want an easy, no-fuss melt and dip.
- Only dip a few cookies at a time before adding peppermint so the chocolate doesn't set before decorating.

CHOCOLATE PEPPERMINT DIPPED BISCUITS

Rich chocolatey, and finished with a festive twist, these Chocolate Peppermint Dipped biscuits are a holiday favourite that never goes out of style. Crisp chocolate biscuits are dipped in smooth white chocolate and sprinkled with crushed peppermint candy canes for a beautiful contrast of flavour and texture. These biscuits are ideal for adding to holiday cookie trays, packaging up as edible gifts, or enjoying alongside a warm drink on a winter afternoon. Simple, striking, and delicious—they're everything a holiday treat should be.

EASTER LEMON GLAZED COOKIES

Ingredients:

- For the Cookies

- 225g unsalted butter, softened

- 100g powdered sugar (¾ cup)

- Zest of 1 lemon

- 1 tsp vanilla extract

- 300g all-purpose flour (2½ cups)

- ¼ tsp fine sea salt

- For the Glaze

- 200g powdered sugar (1½ cups)

- 2-3 tbsp lemon juice

- Gel food coloring (pastels: pink, lavender, yellow, mint green)

- Optional: Sprinkles, edible flowers, or sanding sugar

Directions:

1. Make the Cookies
2. Cream butter, powdered sugar, and lemon zest until light and fluffy.
3. Add vanilla extract and mix.
4. Stir in flour and salt until combined.
5. Roll dough into small balls, flatten slightly, or roll and cut out egg shapes.
6. Chill for 10 minutes.
7. Bake at 350°F (175°C) for 10-12 minutes until edges are just golden. Cool completely.
8. Step 2: Make the Glaze
9. Mix powdered sugar with lemon juice until smooth and pourable.
10. Divide into bowls and tint each with pastel food coloring.
11. Step 3: Dip and Decorate
12. Dip the top of each cookie into the glaze.
13. Add sprinkles, edible flowers, or sanding sugar while glaze is wet.
14. Let dry completely on a wire rack (about 1 hour).

Tips
- Zest the lemon directly over the sugar to capture all the essential oils and maximize flavor.
- For a smooth glaze, sift the powdered sugar before mixing with lemon juice.
- Use gel food coloring for pastel shades—it's more concentrated and won't thin out the glaze.
- Dip the cookies once for a thin glaze or twice for a thicker, more opaque finish. Let dry between dips.

EASTER LEMON GLAZED COOKIES

These Easter Lemon Glazed Cookies are the essence of spring: light, bright, and bursting with fresh citrus flavour. Soft, buttery cookies are infused with lemon zest, then dipped in a delicate pastel glaze for a pop of colour. Simple to make and stunning to display, they're perfect for Easter gatherings, springtime brunches, or as a thoughtful gift wrapped in ribbon. Decorate with sprinkles or edible flowers to make them as festive or elegant as the occasion calls for—these are cookies that taste as good as they look.

LINZER WINDOW COOKIES

Ingredients:

- 225g unsalted butter, softened
- 100g powdered sugar (¾ cup)
- 1 tsp vanilla extract
- 300g all-purpose flour (2½ cups)
- ¼ tsp fine sea salt
- 150g raspberry or strawberry jam
- Powdered sugar for dusting

Directions:

1. Make the Biscuits
2. Cream butter and powdered sugar until light and fluffy.
3. Add vanilla extract.
4. Stir in flour and salt until a dough forms.
5. Roll out dough to 6mm (¼ inch) thick. Cut out rounds and use a smaller cutter to make "windows" in half of them.
6. Chill cut-outs for 10 minutes.
7. Bake at 350°F (175°C) for 10–12 minutes until lightly golden. Cool completely.
8. Step 2: Assemble
9. Spread a small spoonful of jam on each solid cookie base.
10. Top with a window cookie and press gently.
11. Dust tops generously with powdered sugar.

Tip

- Chill the dough after rolling and before cutting to prevent sticking and keep edges sharp.
- Dust the top cookie layer with powdered sugar before assembling to avoid getting sugar on the jam.
- Use a thick jam to prevent it from oozing out the sides.

LINZER WINDOW BISCUITS (EASY VERSION)

Elegant and timeless, these Linzer Window Biscuits strike the perfect balance between buttery richness and fruity sweetness. Two tender, almond-enriched biscuits are sandwiched with jewel-like raspberry or strawberry jam, their signature cut-out windows revealing a glimpse of the filling beneath. A snowy dusting of icing sugar adds the final festive touch.

SNOWBALL COOKIES (RUSSIAN TEA CAKES)

Ingredients:

- 225g unsalted butter, softened
- 100g powdered sugar (¾ cup), plus extra for rolling
- 1 tsp vanilla extract
- 280g all-purpose flour (2¼ cups)
- ½ tsp fine sea salt
- 120g finely chopped pecans or walnuts (1 cup)

Directions:

1. Cream the butter and powdered sugar until smooth and fluffy.
2. Add vanilla extract and mix well.
3. Stir in flour and salt until combined.
4. Fold in chopped nuts until evenly distributed.
5. Roll dough into 2.5cm (1-inch) balls and place on parchment-lined baking sheets.
6. Chill for 15 minutes.
7. Bake at 325°F (160°C) for 12-14 minutes, until just golden on the bottom.
8. Cool slightly, then roll warm cookies in powdered sugar.
9. Once completely cool, roll in powdered sugar a second time for a snowy finish.

Tips

- Finely chop the nuts for the best texture. Large chunks can make the cookies crumbly instead of tender.
- Roll the cookies in powdered sugar twice—once while warm (so the sugar sticks), and again when completely cool for a perfect snowy coating.
- These cookies freeze beautifully. Freeze baked cookies (without sugar coating) and roll them in powdered sugar after thawing.
- Use good quality butter for the richest flavour, since butter is the star ingredient here.

SNOWBALL COOKIES (RUSSIAN TEA CAKES)

These Snowball Cookies are the ultimate holiday classic—tender, buttery morsels that melt in your mouth and are coated in a delicate dusting of powdered sugar. Sometimes known as Mexican Wedding Cookies or Russian Tea Cakes, they're a timeless favourite for festive gatherings and gifting. Simple, elegant, and satisfying, these little treats bring joy to every holiday table.

WORLD-FAMOUS COOKIES: ICONIC RECIPES FROM THE BEST BAKERIES AND BEYOND

Some biscuits are more than just sweet treats—they're legends. These iconic bakes have left their mark on bustling city bakeries, cosy countryside kitchens, and grand patisseries around the world. This chapter celebrates the most beloved and time-honoured biscuits—timeless classics that have found a place in hearts and homes from New York to Paris, Sydney to Vienna.

Here, you'll find easy-to-follow recipes inspired by the biscuits that have stood the test of time. Think chunky, gooey chocolate chip cookies made famous by New York's Levain Bakery; sweet, golden Anzac biscuits steeped in Australian history; or delicate Viennese whirls gracing British afternoon teas. Each recipe captures its origin's flavour, nostalgia, and spirit—with simplified methods to make them accessible to every home baker.

Whether you're recreating a favourite from your travels or discovering a new classic, these recipes invite you to bake a little piece of the world, right from your kitchen.

WORLD-FAMOUS COOKIES: ICONIC RECIPES FROM THE BEST BAKERIES AND BEYOND

Whether you're craving the crisp, caramelized edges of a French Florentine, the rich nuttiness of Mexican Wedding Cookies, or the light lemony sponge of a classic Madeleine, this collection is your passport to world-famous flavors. Perfect for special occasions, gifting, or simply indulging in a moment of nostalgia, these cookies offer something for everyone.

PEANUT BUTTER BLOSSOMS (USA)

Ingredients:

- 125g unsalted butter, softened (½ cup)
- 100g granulated sugar (½ cup), plus extra for rolling
- 100g light brown sugar (½ cup)
- 1 large egg
- 1 tsp vanilla extract
- 130g creamy peanut butter (½ cup)
- 190g all-purpose flour (1½ cups)
- ½ tsp baking soda
- ¼ tsp baking powder
- Pinch of salt
- 24 chocolate kisses (unwrapped)

Directions:

1. Preheat oven to 180°C (350°F). Line baking trays with parchment paper.
2. Cream butter, granulated sugar, and brown sugar until light and fluffy.
3. Beat in the egg, vanilla, and peanut butter until smooth.
4. In a separate bowl, whisk together flour, baking soda, baking powder, and salt.
5. Gradually add dry ingredients to wet, mixing until a soft dough forms.
6. Roll dough into 1-inch (2.5cm) balls and roll in extra granulated sugar.
7. Place on trays 2 inches apart and bake for 8-10 minutes, until golden but soft.
8. Immediately press a chocolate kiss into the center of each cookie. Cool on trays.

PEANUT BUTTER BLOSSOMS (USA)

Created in the American heartland, these soft peanut butter cookies topped with a chocolate kiss have become a beloved staple at cookie swaps, holiday gatherings, and family kitchens across the country. Simple, nostalgic, and delicious, they're an American classic.

BLACK AND WHITE COOKIES (NEW YORK, USA)

Ingredients:

- For the Cookies
- 200g all-purpose flour (1½ cups)
- 1 tsp baking powder
- ¼ tsp baking soda
- ½ tsp fine sea salt
- 100g unsalted butter, softened (½ cup)
- 150g granulated sugar (¾ cup)
- 1 large egg
- 1 tsp vanilla extract
- 120ml buttermilk (½ cup)
- For the Icing
- 250g powdered sugar (2 cups)
- 3-4 tbsp milk or water
- 1 tsp vanilla extract
- 50g dark chocolate, melted (optional: 1 tsp corn syrup for shine)

Directions:

1. Make the Cookies
2. Preheat oven to 180°C (350°F). Line trays with parchment paper.
3. Whisk flour, baking powder, baking soda, and salt in a bowl.
4. In a large bowl, cream butter and sugar until light and fluffy.
5. Add egg and vanilla extract; mix well.
6. Alternately add flour mixture and buttermilk, mixing gently until combined.
7. Drop 2-tablespoon portions onto trays, spacing apart (they will spread).
8. Bake for 10-12 minutes until golden and springy to the touch. Cool completely.
9. Make the Icing
10. Mix powdered sugar, vanilla, and 2 tablespoons of milk into a thick glaze. Add more milk as needed.
11. Frost half the flat side of each cookie with vanilla glaze.
12. Melt chocolate and stir in 1 tablespoon of the vanilla glaze and corn syrup (optional for shine).
13. Frost the other half with the chocolate glaze. Let set for 1 hour.

BLACK AND WHITE COOKIES (NEW YORK, USA)

The Black and White Cookie is a New York City bakery staple, believed to have originated in the early 1900s at Glaser's Bake Shop (now closed) in Manhattan. With its thick, cake-like base and half-and-half icing—vanilla on one side, chocolate on the other—it's more than a cookie. It's a symbol of balance and unity, even featured in Seinfeld's famous line: "Look to the cookie!"

WHOOPIE PIES (AMISH COUNTRY / NEW ENGLAND, USA)

Ingredients:

- For the Cakes
- 250g all-purpose flour (2 cups)
- 75g unsweetened cocoa powder (¾ cup)
- 1½ tsp baking soda
- ½ tsp fine sea salt
- 115g unsalted butter, softened (½ cup)
- 200g brown sugar (1 cup, packed)
- 1 large egg
- 1 tsp vanilla extract
- 240ml buttermilk (1 cup)
- For the Filling
- 120g unsalted butter, softened (½ cup)
- 160g powdered sugar (1¼ cups)
- 1 tsp vanilla extract
- 120g marshmallow fluff (½ cup)

Directions:

1. Make the Cakes
2. Preheat oven to 180°C (350°F). Line trays with parchment paper.
3. In a bowl, whisk flour, cocoa, baking soda, and salt.
4. In a large bowl, cream butter and brown sugar until fluffy.
5. Add egg and vanilla extract; mix well.
6. Alternately add flour mixture and buttermilk to the wet ingredients, mixing gently.
7. Drop batter by heaping tablespoons onto trays, spacing apart.
8. Bake for 10–12 minutes until set and springy. Cool completely.
9. Make the Filling
10. Beat butter and powdered sugar until light and fluffy.
11. Add marshmallow fluff and vanilla extract. Beat until smooth.
12. Assemble
13. Spread or pipe filling onto the flat side of one cake.
14. Top with another cake, pressing gently to sandwich.
15. Optional: Roll edges in sprinkles for a fun finish!

WHOOPIE PIES (AMISH COUNTRY / NEW ENGLAND, USA)

Soft chocolate cake-like cookies sandwiched around a fluffy vanilla filling, Whoopie Pies are the ultimate comfort food. With their origins in Amish country and New England bakeries, they've become a beloved American treat. Perfect for parties, lunchboxes, or indulgent afternoon snacks, these classic pies are sure to bring a little joy to your day.

ANZAC BISCUITS
(AUSTRALIA)

Ingredients:

- 150g rolled oats (1½ cups)
- 150g plain flour (1 cup)
- 100g desiccated coconut (1 cup)
- 100g brown sugar (½ cup)
- 125g unsalted butter (½ cup)
- 2 tbsp golden syrup
- 1 tsp baking soda
- 2 tbsp boiling water

Directions:

1. Preheat oven to 160°C (325°F). Line baking trays with parchment paper.
2. Combine oats, flour, coconut, and sugar in a large bowl.
3. Melt butter and golden syrup in a saucepan over low heat.
4. Dissolve baking soda in boiling water and stir into the butter mixture.
5. Pour wet mixture into dry ingredients and stir well.
6. Roll into balls (about 1 tablespoon each) and flatten slightly on baking trays.
7. Bake for 12–15 minutes until golden brown. Cool on trays before storing.

ANZAC BISCUITS (AUSTRALIA)

These classic Anzac Biscuits are a beloved taste of Australia. Originally baked and sent by loved ones to soldiers during World War I, they're chewy, sweet, and full of oats, coconut, and golden syrup. Easy to make and even easier to love, they keep well, making them perfect for gifting or snacking.

FLORENTINES
(FRANCE/ITALY)

Ingredients:

- 100g flaked almonds (1 cup)
- 75g mixed candied peel (½ cup), finely chopped
- 75g dried cranberries (½ cup), finely chopped
- 50g unsalted butter (¼ cup)
- 50g light brown sugar (¼ cup)
- 50g golden syrup or honey (2 tbsp)
- 75g dark chocolate, melted (½ cup)

Directions:

1. Preheat oven to 180°C (350°F). Line trays with parchment.
2. Mix almonds, candied peel, and cranberries in a bowl.
3. Melt butter, brown sugar, and golden syrup in a pan.
4. Pour over the fruit and nuts; mix to coat evenly.
5. Drop teaspoonfuls onto trays, spaced apart. Flatten slightly.
6. Bake for 8-10 minutes until golden. Cool on trays.
7. Once cool, spread melted chocolate on the flat side. Let set.

FLORENTINES (FRANCE/ITALY)

These classic French Madeleines are light, buttery sponge cakes with a delicate crumb and a signature shell shape. Lightly scented with lemon and dusted with powdered sugar, they're elegant, simple, and perfect for a teatime treat. Enjoy them fresh from the oven with a cup of tea or coffee, just like in the patisseries of Paris.

TATE'S-STYLE THIN & CRISPY CHOCOLATE CHIP COOKIES (USA)

Ingredients:

- 225g unsalted butter, melted (1 cup)
- 200g light brown sugar (1 cup, packed)
- 100g granulated sugar (½ cup)
- 2 large eggs
- 1½ tsp vanilla extract
- 300g all-purpose flour (2½ cups)
- 1 tsp baking soda
- ½ tsp salt
- 300g semi-sweet chocolate chips (2 cups)

"For the perfect crisp bite and caramelised edges, use melted butter, skip chilling the dough, and finish with a sprinkle of flaky sea salt to balance the sweet and buttery richness."

Directions:

1. Preheat oven to 175°C (350°F). Line baking sheets with parchment.
2. In a bowl, mix melted butter, brown sugar, and granulated sugar until combined.
3. Add eggs and vanilla; stir until smooth.
4. In another bowl, whisk flour, baking soda, and salt. Add to wet mixture and stir until blended.
5. Fold in chocolate chips.
6. Drop tablespoonfuls of dough spaced well apart on trays. Flatten slightly.
7. Bake for 10–12 minutes until golden and crisp. Cool on racks.

What makes these cookies different from a traditional chocolate chip cookie is their ultra-thin, crisp, and buttery texture, paired with a deep caramelised flavour.

TATE'S-STYLE THIN & CRISPY CHOCOLATE CHIP COOKIES (USA)

Inspired by the famous Tate's Bake Shop in the Hamptons, these Thin & Crispy Chocolate Chip Cookies are all about buttery crunch and rich chocolate flavour. Their delicate texture and deep caramelized taste make them irresistible. Perfect with a glass of milk or tucked into gift tins, they're a classic American cookie with wide appeal.

FRENCH MADELEINES
(FRANCE)

Ingredients:

- 120g unsalted butter, melted and cooled (½ cup)
- 100g granulated sugar (½ cup)
- 2 large eggs
- 1 tsp vanilla extract
- Zest of 1 lemon
- 120g plain flour (1 cup)
- ½ tsp baking powder
- Powdered sugar, for dusting
- Butter and flour for greasing the mould

Directions:

1. Grease and flour a Madeleine pan.
2. In a bowl, beat eggs and sugar until pale and fluffy (about 5 minutes).
3. Add vanilla and lemon zest.
4. Sift in flour and baking powder. Fold gently to combine.
5. Fold in cooled melted butter until smooth.
6. Cover and chill batter for 30 minutes.
7. Preheat oven to 190°C (375°F).
8. Spoon batter into the moulds (about ¾ full).
9. Bake for 8-10 minutes until golden and domed.
10. Cool slightly, then dust with powdered sugar before serving.

FRENCH MADELEINES (FRANCE)

These classic French Madeleines are light, buttery sponge cakes with a delicate crumb and a signature shell shape. Lightly scented with lemon and dusted with powdered sugar, they're elegant, simple, and perfect for a teatime treat. Enjoy them fresh from the oven with a cup of tea or coffee, just like in the patisseries of Paris.

VIENNESE WHIRLS (UNITED KINGDOM)

Ingredients:

- For the Biscuits
- 250g unsalted butter, softened
- 50g powdered sugar (½ cup)
- 250g plain flour (2 cups)
- 50g cornstarch (½ cup)
- 1 tsp vanilla extract
- For the Filling
- 100g unsalted butter, softened
- 200g powdered sugar (1½ cups)
- ½ tsp vanilla extract
- 100g raspberry jam (or your favourite)

Directions:

1. Preheat oven to 180°C (350°F). Line baking trays with parchment paper.
2. Beat butter, powdered sugar, and vanilla until pale and fluffy.
3. Sift flour and cornstarch into the bowl and mix until smooth.
4. Spoon into a piping bag fitted with a large star nozzle.
5. Pipe 5cm (2-inch) swirls onto trays, leaving room to spread.
6. Chill trays for 10 minutes, then bake for 12-15 minutes until pale golden. Cool completely.
7. For the filling, beat butter, powdered sugar, and vanilla until light and fluffy.
8. Spread or pipe buttercream on half the biscuits. Add a small spoon of jam and sandwich with another biscuit.
9. Dust with powdered sugar before serving.

VIENNESE WHIRLS (UNITED KINGDOM)

Elegant and buttery, these Viennese Whirls are a British teatime favourite. Light and crumbly with a delicate melt-in-your-mouth texture, they're piped into delicate swirls, baked until golden, and sandwiched with vanilla buttercream and raspberry jam. Beautiful to serve and surprisingly easy to make, they bring a touch of charm to any afternoon tea or gift box.

CHUNKY CHOCOLATE CHIP COOKIES (LEVAIN BAKERY, NYC)

Ingredients:

- 225g cold unsalted butter, cubed
- 200g light brown sugar (1 cup, packed)
- 100g granulated sugar (½ cup)
- 2 large eggs
- 1½ tsp vanilla extract
- 400g all-purpose flour (3¼ cups)
- 1 tsp baking powder
- ½ tsp baking soda
- ½ tsp fine sea salt
- 300g semi-sweet chocolate chunks (2 cups)
- 150g toasted walnuts, roughly chopped (1 cup)

Directions:

1. Preheat oven to 190°C (375°F). Line two baking trays with parchment paper.
2. In a large bowl, mix cold butter, brown sugar, and granulated sugar until just combined (not creamed).
3. Add eggs and vanilla extract, mixing until blended.
4. In another bowl, whisk flour, baking powder, baking soda, and salt. Add to the wet mixture and stir until just combined.
5. Fold in chocolate chunks and walnuts.
6. Divide dough into 8 large portions (about 120g each). Shape into rough balls—don't over-roll.
7. Bake for 10–12 minutes until golden brown on the edges, but still soft in the middle. Cool on the tray for 10 minutes before transferring.

CHUNKY CHOCOLATE CHIP COOKIES (LEVAIN BAKERY, NYC)

Inspired by the world-famous Levain Bakery in New York City, these Chunky Chocolate Chip Cookies are everything you dream of in a cookie—crispy golden edges, a soft, gooey center, and packed with chunks of semi-sweet chocolate and toasted walnuts. Oversized and utterly indulgent, they're perfect for sharing… if you can bear to! Whether you've visited the iconic bakery or are experiencing these at home for the first time, this recipe delivers bakery-quality results with simple ingredients and easy steps.

BISCUIT MAGIC:
QUICK & EASY BAKES

Effortless Recipes, Impressive Results

Delicious biscuits that look like they came from a bakery—but come together in no time.

Simple Ingredients

Every recipe uses pantry staples and easy-to-find additions. No hard-to-source items, no fancy tools—just what you already have at home.

Clever Shortcuts

From cake mix hacks to no-bake bars and slice-and-bake doughs, these recipes deliver maximum impact with minimal fuss.

Make-Ahead & Freeze-Friendly

Bake on your schedule! Perfect for busy weeks, last-minute guests, or prepping ahead for special occasions.

Kid-Friendly Fun

Simple steps make these bakes ideal for little helpers—whether you're baking for them or with them.

Elegant Finishes, Minimal Effort

Drizzles, dips, and sprinkles—easy decorating tricks that add a polished, bakery-style finish in minutes.

BISCUIT MAGIC: QUICK & EASY BAKES

Life is busy—but there's always time for a little biscuit magic. In this chapter, you'll find quick and easy recipes designed for busy bakers who want to create something beautiful, delicious, and effortlessly impressive.

From clever cake mix hacks and no-bake delights to slice-and-bake favourites, these recipes are short on time but big on impact. Whether you're pulling together a last-minute dessert tray, filling gift boxes in a hurry, or simply craving a homemade treat without the fuss, these biscuits deliver maximum wow-factor with minimal effort.

No advanced skills required—just simple techniques, clever shortcuts, and plenty of sweet inspiration.

CAKE MIX CRINKLE COOKIES

Ingredients:

- 1 box chocolate cake mix (approx. 425g)
- 2 large eggs
- 60ml (¼ cup) neutral oil (e.g. canola or vegetable)
- 60g (½ cup) powdered sugar, for rolling

Directions:

1. Preheat oven to 175°C (350°F). Line a baking tray with parchment paper.
2. In a large bowl, mix cake mix, eggs, and oil until a sticky dough forms.
3. Scoop tablespoons of dough and roll into balls.
4. Roll each ball generously in powdered sugar.
5. Place on tray, spacing 5cm apart.
6. Bake for 10-12 minutes until cracked and set around the edges.
7. Cool on tray before transferring to a rack.

Tips & Tricks

- Don't overmix the dough—just stir until everything is combined to keep the texture tender.
- For perfectly round cookies, roll the dough balls gently between your palms before coating in powdered sugar.
- Want dramatic cracks? Make sure the dough is well coated in sugar and don't flatten the balls—let them puff naturally.
- Flavour swap: Use red velvet, lemon, or funfetti cake mix for easy variations.
- These freeze beautifully—both the raw dough balls and the baked cookies.

CAKE MIX CRINKLE COOKIES

These soft, fudgy cookies come together in minutes thanks to a clever cake mix shortcut. Rolled in powdered sugar for that signature crackled finish, they're eye-catching, delicious, and almost too easy to be true. A perfect recipe for busy days, last-minute guests, or baking with kids.

NO-BAKE CHOCOLATE PEANUT BUTTER CLUSTERS

Ingredients:

- 200g dark or milk chocolate chips (1¼ cups)
- 120g smooth peanut butter (½ cup)
- 100g quick oats (1 cup)
- 1 tsp vanilla extract
- Pinch of sea salt
- Optional: chopped roasted peanuts or flaky sea salt for topping

Directions:

1. Line a tray with parchment paper.
2. Melt chocolate and peanut butter together in a saucepan or microwave, stirring until smooth.
3. Stir in oats, vanilla, and salt.
4. Drop heaped spoonfuls onto the tray and flatten slightly.
5. Sprinkle with chopped peanuts or sea salt if using.
6. Chill in the fridge for 30 minutes until set.

Tips & Tricks

- Use quick oats, not rolled oats—they absorb better and help the cookies hold their shape.
- Microwave the chocolate and peanut butter in short bursts, stirring between each to avoid burning.
- For more texture, mix in crushed pretzels, shredded coconut, or rice bubbles.
- Sprinkle flaky sea salt on top while still warm for that sweet-salty flavour lift.
- Store in the fridge for a firmer bite, or at room temperature for a softer, chewier texture.

NO-BAKE CHOCOLATE PEANUT BUTTER CLUSTERS

These chewy, chocolatey clusters are the ultimate in no-bake bliss—ready in under 15 minutes with just a handful of pantry staples. Perfect for satisfying cravings fast or whipping up edible gifts on the fly. No oven, no fuss, all flavour.

SLICE-AND-BAKE ALMOND SUGAR BISCUITS

Ingredients:

- 225g unsalted butter, softened
- 100g powdered sugar (¾ cup)
- 1 tsp almond extract
- 270g all-purpose flour (2¼ cups)
- ¼ tsp fine sea salt
- Optional: sanding sugar or melted chocolate for decorating

Directions:

1. Beat butter and sugar until smooth and creamy.
2. Add almond extract and salt, then mix in flour until dough forms.
3. Shape into a log about 5cm (2 inches) in diameter. Wrap in cling film and chill for at least 1 hour.
4. Preheat oven to 175°C (350°F).
5. Slice chilled dough into 1cm rounds. Optional: press edges into sanding sugar.
6. Place on parchment-lined tray and bake for 10–12 minutes until edges are lightly golden.
7. Cool before decorating or serving.

Tips & Tricks

- Shape the dough log as evenly as possible for consistent slices—roll it in parchment like a sushi mat to smooth it out.
- Chill the dough well—it makes slicing easier and prevents cookies from spreading too much.
- Roll the log in sanding sugar or crushed nuts before slicing for a textured, decorative edge.
- These cookies freeze perfectly—wrap the dough log tightly and freeze for up to 2 months.

Add a touch of citrus zest

SLICE-AND-BAKE ALMOND SUGAR BISCUITS

These buttery sugar cookies are the definition of make-ahead magic. Keep a log of dough in the fridge or freezer, slice, bake, and you've got elegant, golden-edged cookies in minutes. Dress them up with sanding sugar or a drizzle of chocolate for effortless sophistication.

MAGIC LAYER BARS (A.K.A. SEVEN-LAYER BARS)

Ingredients:

- 150g (1½ cups) graham cracker crumbs (or digestive biscuit crumbs)
- 85g (6 tbsp) unsalted butter, melted
- 200g (1¼ cups) semi-sweet chocolate chips
- 100g (¾ cup) butterscotch chips (or white chocolate chips)
- 100g (1 cup) sweetened shredded coconut
- 120g (1 cup) chopped walnuts or pecans
- 1 can (400g / 14 oz) sweetened condensed milk

Directions:

1. Preheat oven to 175°C (350°F). Line a 20x20cm (8-inch) square baking tin with parchment paper.
2. In a small bowl, combine the graham cracker crumbs and melted butter. Press firmly into the bottom of the tin to form a base.
3. Layer the chocolate chips, butterscotch chips, shredded coconut, and chopped nuts evenly over the crust.
4. Pour the sweetened condensed milk evenly over the top—do not stir.
5. Bake for 25–30 minutes, or until the edges are golden and the centre is set.
6. Cool completely in the tin before slicing into bars.

Tips & Tricks

- Press the crust firmly into the pan to prevent it from crumbling when sliced. Use the bottom of a glass or measuring cup for even pressure.
- For neat bars, cool completely before slicing, and use a warm, sharp knife for clean cuts.
- Swap the chocolate chips or nuts to suit what you have on hand—these are endlessly customisable.
- Want a twist? Add crushed pretzels to the crust or a pinch of sea salt on top for a sweet-salty upgrade.

MAGIC LAYER BARS (A.K.A. SEVEN-LAYER BARS)

These crowd-pleasing cookie bars are the definition of throw-it-together magic. With just a few pantry staples and no mixing required, they deliver gooey, golden layers of buttery crumbs, chocolate, coconut, and nuts—all brought together by sweetened condensed milk. They're rich, chewy, and endlessly customisable, making them perfect for parties, gifting, or when you need a quick wow-factor treat.

CONFETTI-DIPPED COOKIES

Ingredients:

- 20–24 crisp store-bought vanilla or butter cookies (round or rectangular)
- 200g (1 cup) white chocolate melts or chips
- 80g (½ cup) rainbow sprinkles or pastel confetti
- Optional: edible glitter or sanding sugar for extra sparkle

Directions:

1. Line a tray with parchment paper.
2. Melt white chocolate in a microwave-safe bowl in 30-second bursts, stirring until smooth.
3. Dip one end (or half) of each cookie into the melted chocolate.
4. Immediately dip or sprinkle with confetti/sprinkles.
5. Place on the parchment-lined tray and let set at room temperature for about 30 minutes.

Tps

- Use white candy melts if you want the chocolate to set quickly without tempering.
- For an extra luxe finish, add a touch of edible gold leaf or shimmer dust to the chocolate before it sets.
- Swap in dark or milk chocolate and use gold, silver, or metallic sprinkles for a grown-up version.
- Store in an airtight container for 3–4 days—perfect for party prep!

CONFETTI-DIPPED COOKIES

These cheerful little treats prove that store-bought shortcuts can still feel special. Crisp vanilla cookies are dipped in creamy white chocolate and rolled in colourful confetti or sprinkles. Perfect for birthdays, baby showers, party favours, or whenever you need something sweet and celebratory with minimal effort.

CHOCOLATE RICE BUBBLE CLUSTERS

Ingredients:

- 200g (1¼ cups) dark or milk chocolate, chopped or in chips
- 100g (4 cups) puffed rice cereal (Rice Bubbles/Rice Krispies)
- 1 tsp vanilla extract
- Optional: 30g (2 tbsp) butter or coconut oil for added shine and softness
- Optional toppings: freeze-dried raspberries, crushed nuts, or sprinkles

Directions:

1. Line a tray with parchment or fill mini cupcake liners in a tin.
2. Melt chocolate (and butter or oil, if using) in a microwave or double boiler until smooth.
3. Stir in vanilla, then add puffed rice and gently fold to coat evenly.
4. Scoop spoonfuls onto the tray or into liners.
5. Sprinkle with your chosen toppings.
6. Chill in the fridge for 30–45 minutes until firm. Store in the fridge.

Tips & Tricks
- Use dark chocolate for a richer, more grown-up flavour—or milk chocolate for a classic, nostalgic feel.
- Try white chocolate + crushed freeze-dried strawberries for a pretty twist.
- These are great for making with kids—minimal mess and fun to decorate.
- Keep chilled until serving for the best texture, especially in warm weather.

CHOCOLATE RICE BUBBLE CLUSTERS

A nostalgic favourite with a grown-up twist, these no-bake chocolate clusters are crispy, crunchy, and completely addictive. Made with puffed rice and melted chocolate, they come together in minutes and are perfect for entertaining, gifting, or after-school snacks. No oven required—just melt, mix, and chill!

MARSHMALLOW SANDWICH COOKIES

Ingredients:

- 115g unsalted butter, softened (½ cup)
- 100g light brown sugar (½ cup)
- 50g granulated sugar (¼ cup)
- 1 large egg
- 1 tsp vanilla extract
- 150g all-purpose flour (1¼ cups)
- ½ tsp baking soda
- Pinch of salt
- For the Filling
- 120g marshmallow fluff (about 1 cup)
- Optional: sprinkles, mini chocolate chips, crushed freeze-dried berries

Directions:

1. Preheat oven to 175°C (350°F). Line trays with parchment paper.
2. Cream butter and both sugars until light and fluffy.
3. Beat in the egg and vanilla.
4. Stir in flour, baking soda, and salt until just combined.
5. Scoop small balls of dough (about 1 tablespoon each) and space 5cm apart on trays.
6. Bake for 8-10 minutes until lightly golden on the edges. Let cool completely.
7. Spread or pipe marshmallow fluff onto the flat side of half the cookies.
8. Top with remaining cookies and press gently to sandwich.
9. Roll edges in sprinkles or crushed toppings, if using.

Tips

- Marshmallow fluff is sticky—use a piping bag or spoon chilled fluff for cleaner sandwiching.
- Want more structure? Chill the sandwiched cookies for 15 minutes before serving.
- Add cocoa powder to the dough for a chocolate version, or sandwich with flavoured fluff or Nutella for a twist.

MARSHMALLOW SANDWICH COOKIES

Soft, chewy cookies filled with gooey marshmallow fluff—these playful little sandwiches are as fun to make as they are to eat. Whether rolled in sprinkles, dipped in chocolate, or left beautifully simple, they're a quick and whimsical treat perfect for parties, gifting, or satisfying your sweet tooth in a hurry.

CHOCOLATE LOVERS' COOKIES FOR THOSE WHO BELIEVE THERE'S NO SUCH THING AS TOO MUCH CHOCOLATE.

This chapter is for the true chocolate devotees—the ones who believe that more is always more when it comes to cocoa. Whether you're drawn to gooey, melt-in-the-middle centres or crisp edges with molten middles, this collection delivers the richest, deepest chocolate flavours in every possible form.

From classic double-chocolate chunk bakes to dark cocoa crinkles and elegant chocolate-dipped shortbreads, these recipes celebrate chocolate in all its moods—bold, bittersweet, silky, spiced, or salted. You'll find cookies that are simple and satisfying, as well as those that lean a little luxe, perfect for dinner parties, gifts, or a quiet evening treat.

Whether you're in the mood for a quick, comforting bake or a showstopper that makes people stop mid-bite, this chapter has something for every craving. These are cookies to be savoured, shared, or kept all to yourself. Prepare to bake with intention—and indulge without apology.

CHOCOLATE LOVERS' COOKIES

Whether you're craving something intensely rich, decadently soft, or luxuriously dipped and drizzled, you'll find your fix right here. These recipes range from quick crowd-pleasers to slow bakes that are worth the wait. Every one is designed to impress and satisfy, whether you're baking for guests or sneaking a warm one straight from the tray.

TRIPLE CHOCOLATE CHUNK COOKIES

Ingredients:

- 225g unsalted butter, softened
- 150g brown sugar (¾ cup, packed)
- 100g granulated sugar (½ cup)
- 2 large eggs
- 1½ tsp vanilla extract
- 300g all-purpose flour (2½ cups)
- 30g cocoa powder (⅓ cup)
- ½ tsp baking soda
- ¼ tsp salt
- 100g dark chocolate chunks
- 100g milk chocolate chunks
- 100g white chocolate chunks

Directions:

1. Preheat oven to 175°C (350°F). Line trays with parchment.
2. Cream butter and sugars until light and fluffy.
3. Add eggs and vanilla. Mix well.
4. Whisk flour, cocoa, baking soda, and salt. Add to wet mixture.
5. Fold in all three types of chocolate chunks.
6. Scoop 2 tbsp portions of dough, roll, and place 5cm apart.
7. Bake 10–12 minutes until edges are set but centres are soft. Cool slightly.

Tips
- Don't overbake—cookies continue to set as they cool.
- Use chopped chocolate instead of chips for bigger, melty pockets.
- Chill dough for 30 mins if you want a thicker cookie.

TRIPLE CHOCOLATE CHUNK COOKIES

Soft, chewy cookies filled with gooey marshmallow fluff—these playful little sandwiches are as fun to make as they are to eat. Whether rolled in sprinkles, dipped in chocolate, or left beautifully simple, they're a quick and whimsical treat perfect for parties, gifting, or satisfying your sweet tooth in a hurry.

DOUBLE CHOCOLATE ESPRESSO COOKIES

Ingredients:

- 225g dark chocolate, chopped
- 115g unsalted butter (½ cup)
- 100g brown sugar (½ cup)
- 50g granulated sugar (¼ cup)
- 2 large eggs
- 1 tsp vanilla extract
- 1 tbsp instant espresso powder
- 100g all-purpose flour (¾ cup)
- ½ tsp baking powder
- ¼ tsp salt

Directions:

1. Melt chocolate and butter together, stir until smooth. Cool slightly.
2. Whisk in sugars, eggs, vanilla, and espresso powder.
3. Stir in flour, baking powder, and salt.
4. Chill for 20 mins. Preheat oven to 175°C (350°F).
5. Scoop and bake for 10–12 minutes. Cool on tray.

Tips
- Use high-quality chocolate for best flavour.
- Espresso enhances the chocolate—use decaf if preferred.
- Chill dough for thicker cookies.

DOUBLE CHOCOLATE ESPRESSO COOKIES

Deep, dark chocolate meets the bold flavour of espresso in these rich, chewy cookies. A grown-up twist on a classic, they're perfect with an after-dinner coffee or as a midday pick-me-up for serious chocolate fans.

SALTED DARK CHOCOLATE SHORTBREAD

Ingredients:

- 225g unsalted butter, softened
- 100g powdered sugar (¾ cup)
- 180g all-purpose flour (1½ cups)
- 30g dark cocoa powder (⅓ cup)
- ½ tsp salt
- Flaky sea salt, for topping

Directions:

1. Beat butter and powdered sugar until smooth.
2. Add flour, cocoa, and salt. Mix until a dough forms.
3. Shape into a log, wrap, and chill for 30 minutes.
4. Preheat oven to 160°C (325°F).
5. Slice into 1cm rounds. Place on tray and bake 12-14 minutes.
6. Sprinkle with sea salt while warm.

Tips
- Don't skip the salt—it balances the richness beautifully.
- For crisp edges, chill the dough well before slicing.
- Dip in chocolate for a luxe finish.

SALTED DARK CHOCOLATE SHORTBREAD

Elegant and unexpected, this buttery shortbread is infused with dark cocoa and finished with a sprinkle of flaky sea salt. Sophisticated and addictive, they're crisp, rich, and perfect for when you want something refined but deeply chocolaty.

CHOCOLATE LAVA COOKIES

Ingredients:

- 115g unsalted butter (½ cup)
- 180g dark chocolate, chopped
- 2 large eggs
- 100g brown sugar (½ cup)
- 50g granulated sugar (¼ cup)
- 1 tsp vanilla extract
- 100g all-purpose flour (¾ cup)
- ½ tsp baking powder
- Pinch of salt
- Optional: extra chocolate chunks for filling

Directions:

1. Preheat oven to 175°C (350°F). Line tray with parchment.
2. Melt butter and chocolate together, cool slightly.
3. Whisk in eggs, sugars, and vanilla.
4. Fold in flour, baking powder, and salt.
5. Scoop dough with a chunk of chocolate in the centre (optional).
6. Bake for 10–11 minutes until just set. Rest briefly before serving.

Tips
- Best served warm—reheat briefly if needed.
- Chill dough slightly for thicker cookies.
- Use high-quality chocolate for a true molten centre.

CHOCOLATE LAVA COOKIES

These gooey-centred cookies are like a handheld molten lava cake. Crisp on the outside, melty in the middle, and made for serious chocolate lovers. Serve warm for ultimate indulgence—no spoon required.

THE ART OF COOKIE GIFTING: ELEGANT PACKAGING & PRESENTATION

Homemade cookies have a unique charm—comforting, nostalgic, and made with love. But when thoughtfully packaged, they transform into truly beautiful gifts. Whether you're wrapping buttery shortbreads, glossy chocolate-dipped biscotti, or whimsical sprinkle-dusted marshmallow sandwiches, the right presentation adds polish and joy to every bite.

In this section, you'll find inspiration and ideas for presenting your cookies with the same care you've taken to bake them. From rustic wraps to luxurious gift boxes, every suggestion is designed to help you showcase your cookies in a way that's simple, stylish, and special.

Little Extras That Make a Big Impact
- Handwritten Notes or Quotes
- Include a tag that says "Baked with love", a favourite baking quote, or even a short poem. Add the cookie name and a sweet message—handwritten always wins.
- Finishing Touches
- A touch of ribbon, a gold sticker, or a pressed flower can elevate even the simplest wrapping. Choose colours and textures that complement the cookie inside (e.g. blush ribbon for vanilla sablés, gold twine for festive spiced stars).
- Flavour Pairings
- Attach a tea bag with almond shortbread, a sachet of hot chocolate with crinkle cookies, or a small pot of jam with shortbreads. These thoughtful extras create a full sensory experience.

RUSTIC WRAPS

Rustic Wraps with Parchment & Twine Stack or bundle cookies, wrap in parchment, and secure with baker's twine. Tuck in a sprig of rosemary, lavender, or dried citrus for a charming, homemade feel—ideal for slice-and-bake cookies, Anzac biscuits, or festive gingerbread.

ELEGANT TINS

Elegant Tins & Keepsake Boxes Line a decorative tin or tea caddy with wax paper and fill with cookies that travel well, like snowballs, florentines, or Viennese whirls. Add a silk ribbon and a handwritten tag. Bonus: the tin becomes part of the gift.

MINI DESSERT BOXES

Mini Dessert Boxes for Special Bakes For cookies that feel more like individual desserts—lava cookies, whoopie pies, or marshmallow sandwiches—use cupcake-style dessert boxes. Add a mini spoon, napkin, or flavour pairing for a thoughtful touch.

CLASSIC BAKERY BOXES

Classic Bakery Boxes with a Twist White or kraft boxes lined with parchment, tissue, or a lacy paper doily create an instant bakery feel. For extra flair, seal with a personalised sticker, tie with twine or velvet ribbon, and slip in a little note or recipe card.

CELLOPHANE BAGS

Cellophane Bags & Sweet Seals Perfect for party favours or individual gifting, clear cellophane bags let your cookies shine. Fold and seal neatly with double-sided tape, then finish with a custom label, wax seal, or hand-tied ribbon in colours to match the season or theme.

GLASS JARS

Glass Jars & Pantry-Style Gifting Stack crisp cookies like shortbread, biscotti, or confetti-dipped treats in clean glass jars. Add a swing tag or vintage label and tie with twine, raffia, or satin ribbon. These make beautiful hostess gifts or holiday favours.

Gift Tag Phrases & Sweet Sayings

SHORT & SWEET (FOR TAGS, STICKERS, OR LABELS)

- BAKED WITH LOVE
- JUST A LITTLE SOMETHING SWEET
- FROM MY KITCHEN TO YOURS
- SWEET MOMENTS INSIDE
- HOMEMADE, HEARTFELT, AND DELICIOUS
- FOR YOU (AND MAYBE A FRIEND...)
- ONE BITE = INSTANT JOY
- YOU DESERVE THIS
- A TREAT FOR SOMEONE SWEET
- WITH SUGAR, SPICE & EVERYTHING NICE

Charming Biscuit / Cookie Quotes (for cards or inserts)

ELEGANT & HEARTFELT
- "HAPPINESS IS HOMEMADE."
- "COOKIES ARE LOVE YOU CAN EAT."
- "THERE IS NOTHING THAT A WARM COOKIE CAN'T FIX."
- "A HANDMADE COOKIE IS A HANDWRITTEN NOTE IN EDIBLE FORM."
- "IN A WORLD FULL OF TRENDS, COOKIES ARE A CLASSIC."

PLAYFUL & LIGHT-HEARTED
- "YOU CAN'T MAKE EVERYONE HAPPY… YOU'RE NOT A COOKIE."
- "THIS BOX CONTAINS 0% GUILT, 100% JOY."
- "COOKIES: BECAUSE ADULTING IS HARD."
- "CALORIES DON'T COUNT WHEN THEY'RE WRAPPED THIS CUTE."
- "LIFE IS SHORT. EAT THE COOKIE."

Must-Have Utensils for Effortless Cookie Baking

You don't need a professional kitchen to bake beautiful cookies—just a few reliable tools that help you work efficiently, cleanly, and with a little extra flair. These baking essentials are tried, trusted, and guaranteed to elevate your cookie game.

Measuring Cups and Spoons

Measuring Cups & Spoons
 A good set of dry measuring cups and spoons is a non-negotiable. Look for stainless steel or BPA-free plastic with clear markings.

Mixing Bowls

Mixing Bowls (Large & Medium)
 Choose a sturdy set of bowls in various sizes for mixing doughs and prepping ingredients. Stainless steel, ceramic, or glass all work beautifully.

Spatula

Silicone Spatulas & Wooden Spoons
Silicone spatulas are brilliant for scraping bowls clean and folding in chocolate or mix-ins. A classic wooden spoon is perfect for sturdier doughs.

Rolling Pin

For cut-out cookies, shortbread, and slice-and-bake doughs. Choose a smooth wooden or marble version for an elegant touch.

Baking Pans

Baking Trays (Flat & Rimmed)
Heavy-duty, non-stick baking trays help cookies bake evenly and brown beautifully. Line with parchment or silicone mats for effortless release.

Cooling Rack

Wire Cooling Racks
Essential for helping cookies cool quickly and evenly. Keeps bottoms crisp and prevents overbaking once out of the oven.

Cookie Cutters

Great for festive shapes, sandwich cookies, or decorated biscuits. Opt for classic rounds, fluted edges, or themed sets.

Digital Kitchen Scales

Precision matters, especially in baking. A small digital scale helps you measure by weight for better accuracy and consistent results.

GROCERY LIST

Date: _____ Week: _____

GROCERY LIST

Date: _____ Week: _____

GROCERY LIST

Date: _____   Week: _____

Kitchen measurements

CONVERSION CHART

Dry weights

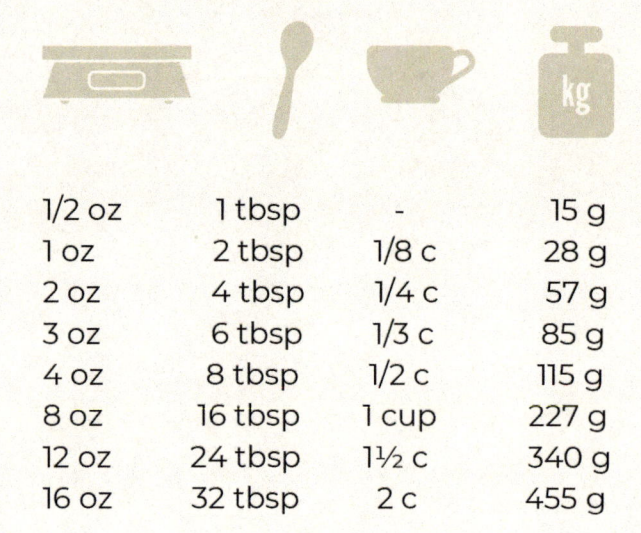

1/2 oz	1 tbsp	-	15 g
1 oz	2 tbsp	1/8 c	28 g
2 oz	4 tbsp	1/4 c	57 g
3 oz	6 tbsp	1/3 c	85 g
4 oz	8 tbsp	1/2 c	115 g
8 oz	16 tbsp	1 cup	227 g
12 oz	24 tbsp	1½ c	340 g
16 oz	32 tbsp	2 c	455 g

Liquid Volumes

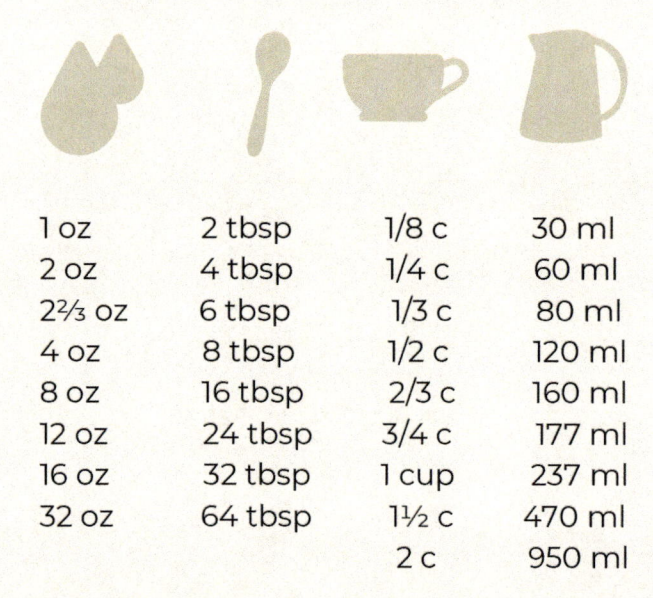

1 oz	2 tbsp	1/8 c	30 ml
2 oz	4 tbsp	1/4 c	60 ml
2⅔ oz	6 tbsp	1/3 c	80 ml
4 oz	8 tbsp	1/2 c	120 ml
8 oz	16 tbsp	2/3 c	160 ml
12 oz	24 tbsp	3/4 c	177 ml
16 oz	32 tbsp	1 cup	237 ml
32 oz	64 tbsp	1½ c	470 ml
		2 c	950 ml

1 oz = 28 grams
1 lbs = 454 g
1 cup = 227 g

1 tsp = 5 ml
1 tbsp = 15 ml
1 oz = 30 ml
1 cup = 237 ml
1 pint = 473 ml (2 cups)
1 gallon = 16 cups

Abbreviations

tbsp = Tablespoon
tsp = Teaspoon
fl.oz – Fluid Ounce
c = cup
ml = Milliliter
lb = pound
F = Fahrenheit
C = Celsius
ml = Milliliter
g = grams
kg = kilogram
l = liter

Oven temperature

130 c = 250 F
165 c = 325 F
177 c = 350 F
190 c = 375 F
200 c = 400 F
220 c = 425 F

A Final Note from Me to You

Thank you for joining me on this sweet journey through the world of beautiful biscuits. Whether you came for a quick bake, a thoughtful gift, or simply a quiet moment in the kitchen, I hope you've found something to make your table more joyful and your day a little sweeter.

These pages were created with care and the belief that even the simplest biscuit—tied with ribbon or shared over tea—can bring people together and turn ordinary moments into something special.

Baking doesn't need to be perfect to be meaningful. A cracked top or uneven swirl is just part of the charm—and a reminder that it was made by hand, with heart.

If this book inspired you to try something new, share a bake, or simply slow down for a moment of joy, then it's done exactly what I'd hoped.

Michelle xoxo

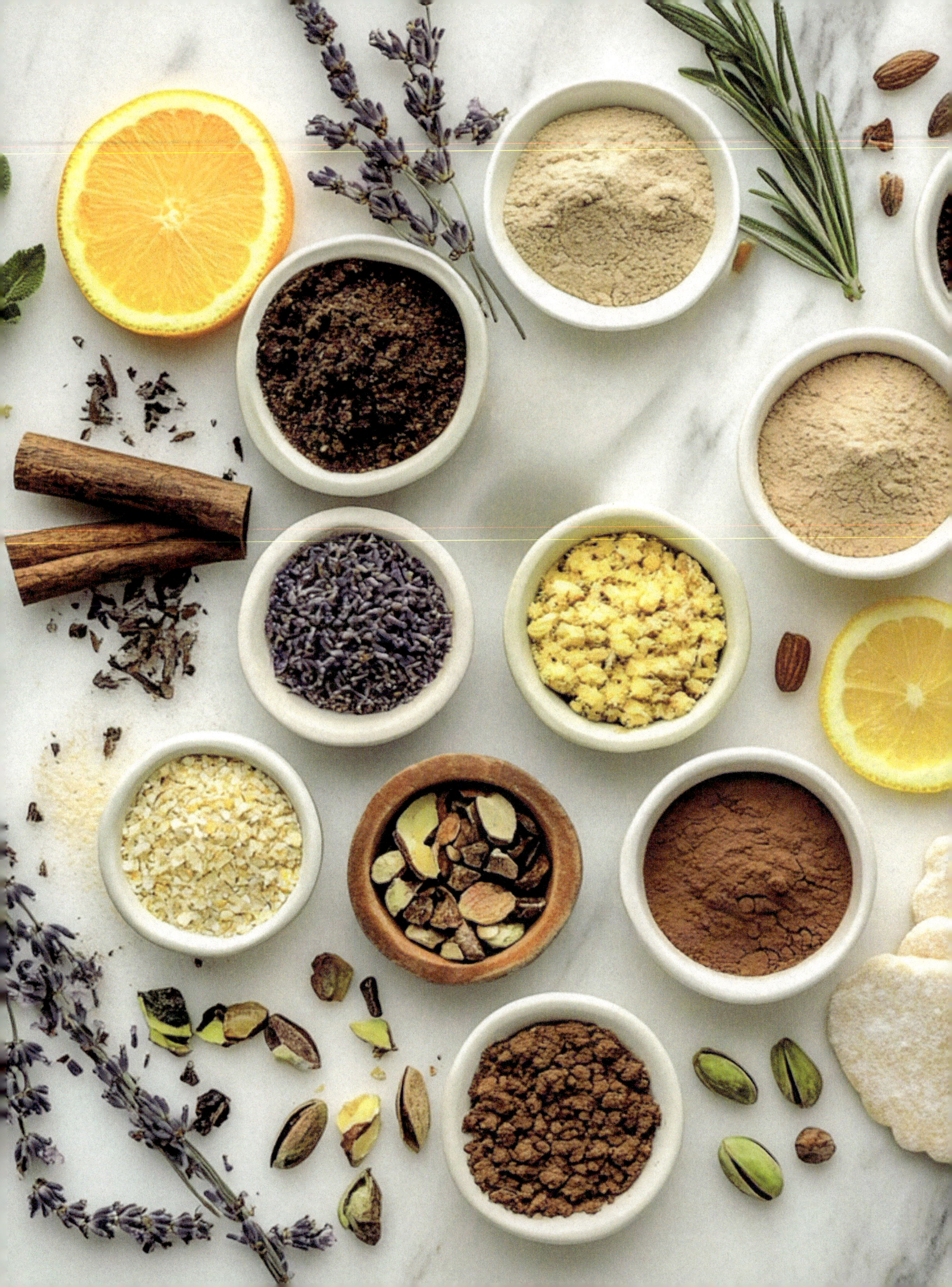

The Sweetest Extras

Mix & Match Flavour Ideas

Create your own signature cookies with simple flavour combinations. Classic shortbread and sugar cookie doughs are the perfect blank canvas. This guide will help you dream up your own variations using ingredients you already love. Just pick a base, add a flavour twist, and finish with a flourish. Sweet, simple, and endlessly customisable.

✨ **Start with a Dough:**
- Classic Vanilla Sugar Cookie
- Classic Buttery Shortbread
- Brown Sugar Shortbread
- Chocolate Sugar Cookie

✨ **Add Flavour:**

Choose one (or two!) of these mix-ins:
- Lemon zest + vanilla bean
- Orange zest + cardamom
- Crushed freeze-dried strawberries
- Chopped pistachios or almonds
- Cocoa nibs + espresso powder
- Coconut + lime zest
- Lavender + honey
- Ground cinnamon or chai spice

✨ **Finish with Flair:**

Try one of these elegant final touches:
- Dip or drizzle with white, dark, or milk chocolate
- Roll edges in sanding sugar, chopped nuts, or sprinkles
- Dust with powdered sugar or edible shimmer
- Press a whole nut, edible flower, or fruit slice on top before baking
- Glaze with citrus icing or tinted glaze for a pop of colour

Tip: You can divide one batch of dough and try a few different combinations. Great for gifting assortments or experimenting with seasonal flavours!

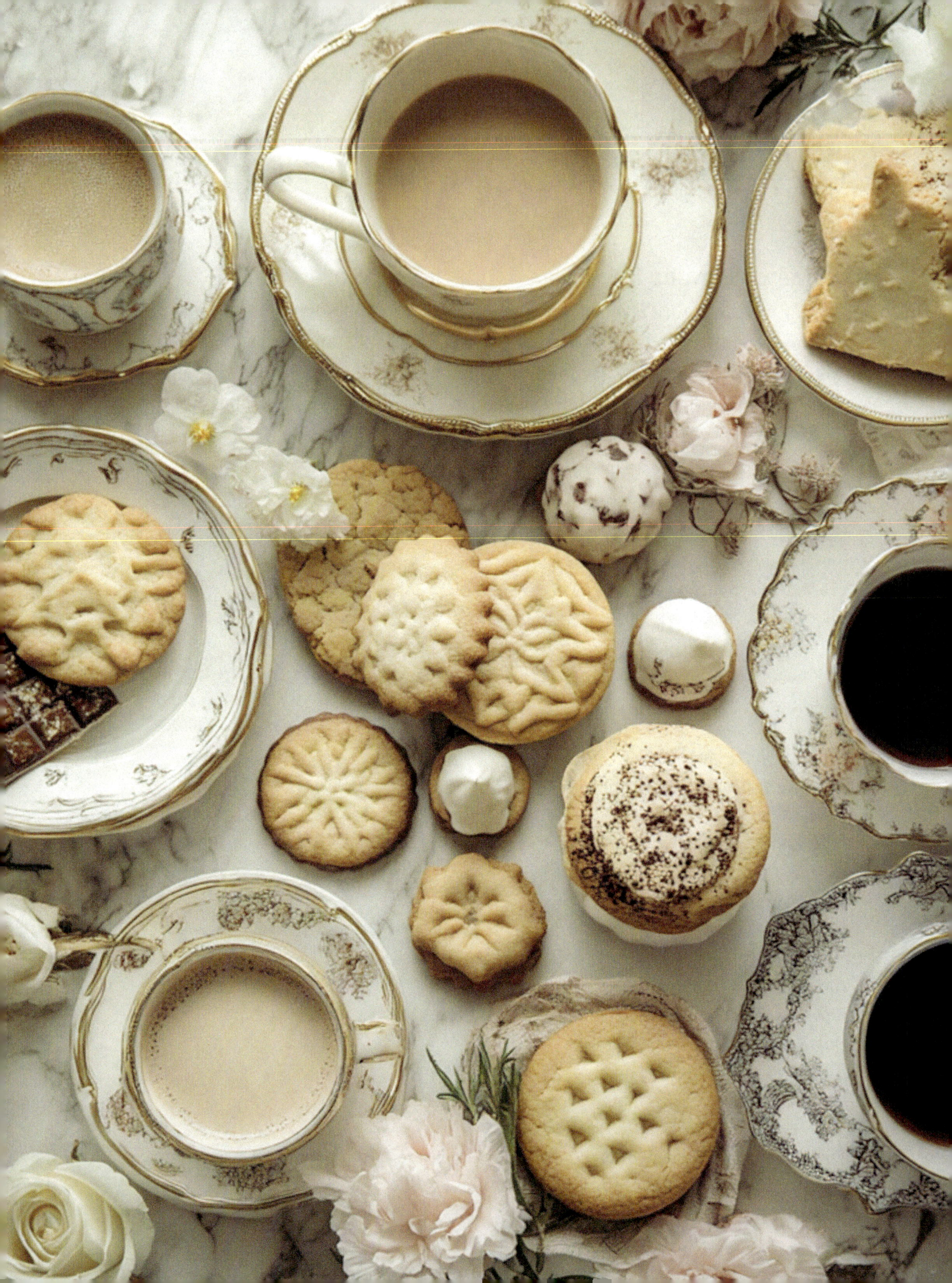

Cookie & Biscuit Tea/Coffee Pairings

Because the right cookie and the perfect cup were made for each other.

Some flavours just belong together—like buttery shortbread melting alongside a delicate tea or a dark chocolate cookie paired with a strong shot of espresso. These pairings aren't just delicious; they elevate the whole experience, turning a simple snack into a ritual.

Enjoy these suggestions for hosting, gifting, or treating yourself to a quiet moment with your favourite bake and a warm cup.

✨ **Classic Combinations**

Almond Shortbread
 It pairs beautifully with: Chamomile or Earl Grey
The buttery texture melts alongside floral and citrus notes.

Viennese Whirls
 Pairs beautifully with Darjeeling or English Breakfast Tea
Delicate, creamy, and softly sweet—a timeless afternoon treat.

Raspberry Window Cookies
 It pairs beautifully with: Green tea or rosehip herbal tea
Fruity and floral, this pairing is light and fragrant.

✨ **For the Chocolate Lovers**

Chocolate Crinkle Cookies
 It pairs beautifully with: Espresso or mocha
Bold, rich and indulgent—this is dessert in a cup and on the plate.

Salted Dark Chocolate Shortbread
 Pairs beautifully with Black coffee or French press
Bittersweet and refined, with just enough edge.

Chocolate-Dipped Biscotti
 Pairs beautifully with a cappuccino or strong latte
Crunchy, creamy, and made for slow sips.

✨ **For Celebrations & Colour**

Confetti-Dipped Cookies
 Pairs beautifully with a vanilla latte or chai tea
Sweet meets spice in the most cheerful way.

Lemon-Glazed Easter Cookies
 Pairs beautifully with Iced tea with honey or green jasmine tea
Bright and refreshing with a subtle citrus zing.

Marshmallow Sandwich Cookies
 Pairs beautifully with: Hot chocolate or spiced milk tea
Whimsical and nostalgic—made for comfort.

Biscuit & Cookie Recipe Index

Page 8 Classic Buttery Shortbread
Page 10 Raspberry Window
Page 12 Pressed Flower Shortbread
Page 14 Pistachio Thumbprint
Page 16 Chocolate Dipped Hazelnut
Page 18 Vanilla Sables
Page 20 Italian Amaretti
Page 22 Lavender Shortbread
Page 26 Marbled Fondant
Page 28 Chocolate Transfer
Page 30 Stained Glass
Page 32 Painted Botanical
Page 34 Confetti Dipped
Page 36 White Chocolate Drizzle
Page 40 Spiced Gingerbread
Page 42 Cinnamon Sugar
Page 44 Chocolate Peppermint
Page 46 Easter Lemon
Page 48 Linzer Window
Page 50 Snowball
Page 54 Peanut Butter
Page 56 Black And White

Biscuit & Cookie Recipe Index

Page 58 Whoopie Pies
Page 60 Anzac
Page 62 Florentines
Page 64 Tate's Style Thin and Crispy
Page 66 French Madeline's
Page 68 Viennese Whirls
Page 70 Chunky Choc Chip
Page 74 Crinkle Cookies
Page 76 No Bake Peanut Clusters
Page 78 Slice And Bake Almond Sugar
Page 80 Magic Layer Bars
Page 82 Confetti Dipped
Page 84 Chocolate Rice Bubbles
Page 86 Marshmallow Sandwich
Page 90 Triple Choc
Page 92 Double Choc Espresso
Page 94 Salted Dark Chocolate
Page 96 Chocolate Lava

Printed in Great Britain
by Amazon